Thank You For The Days

Fans of The Kinks share 60 years of stories

Edited by
Chris Kocher

sonicbondpublishing.com

Sonicbond Publishing Limited
www.sonicbondpublishing.co.uk
Email: info@sonicbondpublishing.co.uk

First Published in the United Kingdom 2024
First Published in the United States 2024

British Library Cataloguing in Publication Data:
A Catalogue record for this book is available from the British Library

Copyright Chris Kocher 2024

ISBN 978-1-78952-342-3

The rights of individual contributors to be identified as the authors
of this work have been asserted by them in accordance with the
Copyright, Designs and Patents Act 1988.

All rights reserved. No part of this publication may be reproduced,
stored in a retrieval system or transmitted in any form or by any means,
electronic, mechanical, photocopying, recording or otherwise, without
prior permission in writing from Sonicbond Publishing Limited

Typeset in ITC Garamond Std & ITC Avant Garde Gothic
Printed and bound in England

Graphic design and typesetting: Full Moon Media

Colour cover photographs: Marianne Spellman.
Black and white photos: Alamy

Follow us on social media:
Twitter: https://twitter.com/SonicbondP
Instagram: www.instagram.com/sonicbondpublishing_/
Facebook: www.facebook.com/SonicbondPublishing/

Linktree QR code:

Thank You For The Days

Fans of The Kinks share 60 years of stories

Edited by
Chris Kocher

sonicbondpublishing.com

Acknowledgements

I appreciate all the incredible Kinks fans and friends who have contributed their stories and photos to this book. Special thanks to Geoff Lewis, Neil Ottenstein, Dave Emlen and Dame Olga Ruocco for their guidance and support.

My wife, Crystal, offered lots of encouragement as the book came together. Love ya, kid.

Thanks to Stephen Lambe and Sonicbond for taking a chance on this idea.

And, of course, eternal gratitude to Ray Davies, Dave Davies, Mick Avory and The Kinks for the great music over the past 60 years. (Fraser Kennedy was instrumental in securing the contributions from the band that appear in this book. Thank you, sir!)

Thank You For The Days

A Few Words From The Band ...

For the community of Kinks fans everywhere, memories of
moments in our lives and the music that has connected us all.
Ray Davies

I think it is really awesome and inspiring to hear the thoughts
and feelings of the fans over the years. It casts an interesting and
different light on The Kinks' legacy. It's cool to uncover these
thoughts and experiences of fans.
Dave Davies

From the very start, I've always been very grateful to fans who
follow the band, some of whom have become friends
over the years, and I still have the opportunity to see
them each year at the Kinks convention.
Mick Avory

Thank You For The Days

Fans of The Kinks share
60 years of stories

Contents

Introduction 11
The 1960s 12
The 1970s 26
The 1980s 43
The 1990s 60
The 2000s 102
The 2010s 117
The 2020s (So Far) 132
Afterword: 2023 133

Introduction

Everyone has a story. Sure, it's a cliché – but I also happen to believe it. Sometimes, the tricky part is coaxing that story out of them. I've been a 'dedicated follower' of The Kinks for almost 30 years now, and I've heard some amazing stories from fellow fans about how the band and their music have shaped our lives. That love has led me on unexpected adventures and forged lifelong connections with folks all over the world.

As The Kinks began celebrations for their 60th anniversary in early 2023, I wondered how I could honour their legacy, too. Brothers Ray and Dave Davies each published two autobiographies of thoughts about their rock-star experiences, and other books (some better than others) have covered the trajectory of their careers. Scholarly authors continue to delve into the meaning behind the music, making connections to history and the wider societal changes that influenced Ray Davies' lyrics.

I realised the one thing that's never been done – at least not in book form – is a collection of the best fan stories. As an editor, I've worked with many people who aren't professional writers to make their pieces better, so I felt like this was the service I could offer to the Kinkdom.

To avoid submissions that read like laundry lists of concerts or personal encounters (which I think would be boring on page after page), I wanted that one best story related to The Kinks – what song hooked them first, the concert that made them a fan, a time when the music gave them joy or solace, how they met their spouse or best friend because of The Kinks, a time they interacted with band members, or something similar. I'd slot the stories chronologically.

I posted the guidelines on social media and on the fan website kindakinks.net, and fans from around the world sent incredible stories about how The Kinks are woven into the fabric of their lives. One escaped East Germany's oppressive regime so he could see the band live. Another met his future wife through an ad in a music magazine as he looked to connect with other Kinks fans, sparking a long-distance romance. Yet, another got to be a Kink for the night, playing an impromptu post-concert set in a hotel bar with a few band members.

To add another dimension to the book, I also reached out to musicians who have been influenced by The Kinks, folks who have collaborated or worked with Ray and Dave Davies over the years and authors of previous books about the band. I'm thrilled to include memories from David Temple (co-founder of the Crouch End Festival Chorus), Wesley Stace (a novelist better known to music fans as John Wesley Harding), Ron Sexsmith (who credits The Kinks for inspiring his songwriting career), Jonathan Lea (sharing his behind-the-scenes account of the Davies brothers' onstage reunion in 2015) and others.

I hope that you enjoy reading this book as much as I enjoyed putting it together. God save The Kinks and all those who love 'em.

Chris Kocher

Thank You For The Days

The 1960s

The origins of it all. Inspired by American blues and rock 'n' roll, brothers Ray (rhythm guitar) and Dave Davies (lead guitar) teamed up with friend Pete Quaife (bass) to form a band they initially called The Ramrods, The Bo-Weevils, or after whichever member booked the gig (such as the Ray Davies Quartet). As The Ravens, they added Mick Avory (drums), acquired management and were renamed The Kinks in 1963. Onstage, their distinctive 'fab gear' included red hunting jackets, frilly shirts, black trousers and Chelsea boots.

After two underperforming singles on Pye Records, 'You Really Got Me' – fuelled by Dave's frenetic, distorted, now-iconic guitar riff – rocketed to number one in the UK charts in September 1964. Follow-ups 'All Day And All Of The Night' and 'Tired Of Waiting For You' (both number two) sealed their powerhouse status.

A disastrous US tour in mid-1965 led the American Federation of Musicians union to ban The Kinks from performing there during the hottest years of the so-called British Invasion. Mick and Ray later attributed the ban to a combination of 'bad luck, bad management and bad behaviour.' The band fired manager Larry Page, which led to a protracted court fight.

Like all creative bands in the hothouse of the 1960s music scene, The Kinks' style and subject matter evolved quickly. Cut off from America, their songs turned inward to British themes and incorporated jauntier music-hall styles. By late 1965, singles such as 'A Well-Respected Man' and 'Dedicated Follower Of Fashion' heralded Ray's turn to satirical subjects, with 'Sunny Afternoon' hitting number one in mid-1966.

'Waterloo Sunset' – frequently hailed as The Kinks' best song – reached number two in the charts in May 1967, but their subsequent album, *Something Else By The Kinks*, proved commercially disappointing. Dave scored a number three hit with 'Death Of A Clown' (also included on *Something Else*).

For 1968's *The Kinks Are The Village Green Preservation Society*, Ray found inspiration in Dylan Thomas' *Under Milk Wood*, drawing lyrical sketches of pastoral life. The album was released on the same day as The Beatles' 'White Album' to wide acclaim from music critics, but it failed to chart in the UK or US. Soon after *Village Green*, Pete left The Kinks lineup and was replaced by John Dalton.

Arthur (Or The Decline And Fall Of The British Empire), released in 1969, was meant to be the soundtrack for a television play for Granada Television developed with novelist Julian Mitchell, but the programme fell through. Ray negotiated an end to the US touring ban, but initial concerts yielded mixed results.

For most British fans (and many Americans who caught up later), these were the glory years.

Albums by The Kinks: *Kinks* (1964), *Kinda Kinks* (1965), *The Kink Kontroversy* (1965), *Face To Face* (1966), *Something Else By The Kinks* (1967),

Live At Kelvin Hall (1968), *The Kinks Are The Village Green Preservation Society* (1968), *Arthur (Or The Decline And Fall Of The British Empire)* (1969)

1963
John Penhallow – Wollongong, New South Wales, Australia
At the tender age of 14, I booked The Ravens to play at a dance for the Methodist Church Youth Club in Muswell Hill, North London, on 23 November 1963, and I sold all the tickets. Between the booking and the show, The Ravens became The Kinks – now clad in their red-wine hunting jackets and frilly white shirts – a few months before they released 'You Really Got Me' for their first number-one hit single.

Then, US President John F. Kennedy was shot in Dallas on 22 November. As Ray Davies wrote in his book *X-Ray*:

> I was convinced that there was going to be a world war. To my relief, Muswell Hill and the rest of the world were still there when we played the Moravian Hall the following night, but the taste of violence and the black-and-white images from Dallas would not leave me.

When I met Ray again outside his house in Highgate in 2015, I told him where we had met before, and he remembered the gig. 'That was you, was it?' he asked. We will never forget it.

There's a line in the *Sunny Afternoon* musical when Pete Quaife is telling Ray he wants to quit the band. He says something like, 'It was more fun when we was playing at the Yoof Club!' I like to think that was our Youth Club back in 1963.

1964
Ian Rhydderch – Swansea, Wales, UK
In 1964, I was ten years old and already a committed fan of pop music. My two older brothers and my parents had a collection of 78 RPM rock 'n' roll and skiffle records and a lovely Ferguson radiogram that I had mastered at the age of three!

My life changed when my father got a promotion and relocated the family to Rotherham in Yorkshire from Newcastle-under-Lyme, Staffordshire, where I was in primary school. I was about to take the 11-plus exam, so my mother and I camped out with family friends in Newcastle until December so I could stay in my old school and take the exam. We commuted over to Rotherham for weekends in my mum's little red Ford Anglia with a three-speed gearbox and no heater!

My prize possession during this time was my little red transistor radio, which was always with me. BBC radio stations were tame back then, and this resulted in the rise of pirate radio. The most important to me was Radio Luxembourg, and I used to listen to DJs such as Simon Dee and Jack Jackson under the bedcovers every night. The sound would fade in and out – but that, somehow, made the music more intriguing. Of course, one band they played was The Kinks. I remember being unconvinced by 'You Really Got Me' at first, but I loved their version of 'Louie Louie', which was frequently played.

On our journeys over to Rotherham, my mum would always stop for a cuppa and ciggie at a truck stop place that had a jukebox. 'All Day And All Of The Night' was released, and suddenly, I was hooked, begging for money and playing it every time we were there. I bought a copy with my pocket money as soon as I could, but I could only play it at home on weekends. I got the EP *Kinksize Session* for my 11th birthday that November (with 'Louie Louie' on it) and the first Kinks album for my Christmas present. Since then, I have bought every piece of music released by The Kinks, Ray and Dave Davies.

I didn't get to see the band play live until 1972, but from that point, I followed them at every turn until the last time in Croydon in 1994. It was always my philosophy to never attempt to meet my heroes, but after reading Ray's autobiography, *X-Ray*, and being moved by what he said, I plucked up the courage to say hello to him after a solo gig in Reading. Since then, I have greeted him at every gig and spent some time with him when I attended his songwriting course in 2017. He is a lovely man, very aware of his talent but generous with his time and always respectful of his fans.

I celebrate the music every November at the annual Kinks Konvention and sing with the Kinksfan Kollektiv at The Clissold Arms in Muswell Hill, an event I cherish. The music is and always will be a part of me. God save The Kinks.

Scott Allardice – Parish, New York, US

It was probably September 1964, a full six months after I watched my two pre-teen sisters scream and squeal at The Beatles on *The Ed Sullivan Show*, and I became convinced of the stupidity of pop music. I was seven years old.

We were travelling north on Rochester's Mount Read Boulevard in our blue 1962 Chevy II. Mom was driving. A sister (I don't recall which one) held the front seat and thus had control of the AM radio with its lone speaker in the dashboard. I was relegated to the back seat, staring out the window. The radio was, of course, tuned to WBBF, Rochester's top 40 station, playing whatever the hits were that week. I ignored it all. Suddenly, those chords rang out. As 'You Really Got Me' played on the radio, I stood up, stuck my head into the front seat and said, 'What's that?!' I've been a fan ever since.

Åke Banksell – Stockholm, Sweden

As a teenager, I bought almost every record by The Kinks on the very first day of release in Sweden. I was 12 years old in 1964, and I believe my blood started to run much faster from the first time I heard 'You Really Got Me'. The next day, I ran to the music shop and found the single.

When I later heard 'All Day And All Of The Night', I put it on my Christmas list, which I regret because I had to wait a very long time before I could play the record. From then on, I was a frequent customer at my record store. Sometimes, the band surprised me with an EP I didn't know about.

Being very addicted to raw rock music, I learnt to like softer styles through The Kinks. 'Tired Of Waiting' and its lack of a guitar solo was a disappointment, but I began to love it eventually, and then other songs, too. My father gave me his old acoustic guitar with only three playable strings, and in time, I learnt many Kinks songs.

Mick Kiff – Grimsby, UK
When I was 13 years old in 1964 and a fan of The Kinks, the headmaster at my school took me to my father's barbershop to get my hair cut and asked why my hair was so long. My father said that I wouldn't get it cut because of The Kinks. Did my hair get cut? No! My mother stopped my dad, and the headmaster wasn't happy. I still have long hair today, and I'm still a fan of The Kinks!

1965
Around The Dial With ... Doug Hinman
On 20 January 1965, I was 11 years old. I had two older brothers, both into music. We religiously watched the TV show *Shindig!* every week. They each had their own favourite artists: The Beatles, The Beach Boys, Chuck Berry, The Rolling Stones and so forth.

Up until that night, I had yet to 'pick' any one group. But on that show, there they were – The Kinks. I'm sure I'd heard their first two hits on the radio, but I took no particular notice. Something about their appearance instantly registered with me: Dave's shockingly long hair, the longest ever at that time, and Ray's odd mannerisms and gap-toothed grin. The whole package just hit me – boom! I had a band that were *my* band. Oddly, I remember remarking when they played their second song ('All Day And All Of The Night') that I thought it was the same as the first one ('You Really Got Me').

That very weekend, I scrounged together the money (79 cents) to buy 'All Day And All Of The Night' at our local TV and record shop. After that, I bought the first Kinks album – my first rock album – which I distinctly remember playing on my father's record console. Initially, I couldn't identify their photos by name, and I had to borrow a British music magazine from my oldest brother that identified them. I carefully wrote their names above their picture on the back cover, which I still have to this day.

I proceeded to follow them on TV and radio, hit after hit, album after album. I recall that I had a legal yellow pad on which I carefully wrote down every television appearance and song they played. I caught them all: *Hullabaloo*, *The Red Skelton Show*, *Shivaree*, *The Lloyd Thaxton Show*, *Where The Action Is* and more *Shindig!* appearances.

Their chart presence wobbled greatly after 'Tired Of Waiting', but I bought every single and album as they came out. They disappeared from television after January 1966, and there was minimal coverage in the teen press – only a few articles in *Hit Parader*. I remember hearing 'Dead End Street' on AM radio but can't recall 'Mr. Pleasant' particularly. One distinct thrill was seeing them on *Piccadilly Palace*, a summer replacement for *Hollywood Palace* in 1967.

By then, music was changing. Early in 1968, FM radio emerged. I could no longer find their singles after 'Autumn Almanac' in the local record stores. I recall reading about Dave's first two singles in *Crawdaddy* in 1968 and asking the older woman at the record store about them. She literally chuckled at the absurdity of my request. I was later surprised to find the *Something Else* LP, but the rock world was rapidly transformed by 1968, and the Kinks were all but invisible that year.

Finally, in December 1968, I read a notice in a local music magazine that there was a new album out in England, *The Village Green Preservation Society*. Figuring it would never come out in the US, I found an address in the back of *Rolling Stone* magazine for 'any British LP $6.50' airmailed from England. They wrote back on 9 January 1969, and I promptly ordered it. This became my prized possession. It was difficult to imagine The Kinks even still existed and with the original lineup to boot.

In the spring, I heard a local DJ casually mention, 'The Kinks have broken up', but I was reluctant to believe it. Finally, in late May, a major album review for the *Village Green* LP appeared in *Rolling Stone* with a prominent picture of the band minus original bassist Pete Quaife and someone else in his place. This was a shock, but it was a rave review, and I felt my years of loyalty were publicly justified.

Soon after, things started to come back to life for the band, and in October, the news: The Kinks would play at the Boston Tea Party. I was just 16 and convinced my mother to drive me to Boston. That was the truly magic moment. They were all real people, and I sat in awe and felt a major victory after a torturously long four-and-a-half-year wait. I saw them again in February and June 1970, but after that, 'Lola' hit and things were never the same, with decades of varying success.

Those memories from the 1960s kept me inspired, though. Long ago, I misplaced that yellow legal pad, but eventually, I went on to write two books about the band and somehow haven't let go to this day.

Hinman has researched and written two definitive books on The Kinks' career: *You Really Got Me – An Illustrated World Discography* and *All Day And All Of The Night: Day By Day Concerts, Recordings, And Broadcasts*. He lives in Warren, Rhode Island.

V. Mary Carroll – Moriarty, New Mexico, US

Saturday, 26 June 1965. Sacramento Memorial Auditorium. Center Section, Row B, Seat 103. My first Kinks concert. I framed the ticket.

Vicki, my partner in crime, nailed the Mod look. My plain graduation dress was adequate. We were giddy on the bus ride into town. We watched The

Kinks' stage gear being unloaded from a chartered coach at the rear of the auditorium. We were lucky – Dave Davies and Mick Avory joined us on the sidewalk! Sam Curtis, The Kinks' road manager, relaxed against a car. A thoughtful equipment handler tore a baggage tag in half, allowing each of us our own Kinks souvenir.

When Mick and Dave mentioned wanting something to drink, Vicki and I escorted them to Sam's Hof Brau, two blocks away. Dave (in a blue gingham shirt, hip-huggers and moccasins) and Mick (in a white corduroy Levi's outfit) puffed on cigarettes. Spotting a piece of fluff floating above us, Dave and I simultaneously reached for it. Our hands collided. His cigarette singed the back of my hand. I felt the burn, but when he asked about it, I fibbed and said I was fine. Mick ordered orange juice. Dave had a Coke.

Back at the auditorium, my pal and I boarded their bus. Dave closed the door. Vicki aimed her camera at him. I snapped my Instamatic 100. The flashbulb didn't go off. Dave's advice: 'Lick the bulb.' I did, but the photo still came out underexposed. I asked him where The Kinks were staying, and he told me. After the concert, Vicki and I flagged a yellow cab.

Some reports from this show claim the 45-minute set included a 20-minute version of 'You Really Got Me' (because of a dispute with the promoter), but I don't recall that. The screaming audience did make listening to The Kinks' performance difficult. I recognised several B-sides. The Kinks wore black jackets, white frilly shirts, grey trousers and black boots. Dave executed a backbend, the top of his head almost touching the stage floor while he continued wailing on his guitar. Appreciative shrieks ripped through the auditorium.

Before the concert, a friend handed her camera to a DJ. She later gave me the backstage photos he snapped. Dave posed with a Guild (the famous Flying V came later). Pete hoisted a Rickenbacker bass. Morose Ray, in shirtsleeves, grasped a Fender. (Circa 1977, I showed Ray this photo. He said he still had the guitar, but he'd painted it blue).

The night morphed into dreamland when we encountered an animated Pete Quaife. He'd been out with a classy lass piloting a sleek black Mustang. After they traded farewells, Prince Charming welcomed us into his room. Pete, 21, handsome and easygoing, caused my heart to flutter. At 17, Vicki and I were both in violation of the 10 pm curfew. We didn't care.

Pete entertained us past the wee hours, discussing his nylon panties mentioned in 'Dedicated Follower Of Fashion'; Ray, not feeling well, preferring to stay in his room; Ray writing 'This Strange Effect' for Dave Berry; Pete's stage shirt being stolen in Los Angeles; and his teen crush on a Suzanne Pleshette look-alike. He signed the sheet music for 'All Day And All Of The Night' that I bought that afternoon. The dog on the cover, he said, was literally mad.

Yawns accompanied Pete to the unlatched door. I asked what he was doing. 'Watching the sunrise', he said, smiling over his shoulder. The sky swirled sherbet orange and pink. Vicki and I collected hugs from a sleepy Pete before we scrambled across the Tower Bridge into town. Vicki got grounded. I didn't.

A week later, on 4 July 1965, I boarded a chartered bus rolling toward San Francisco. Section A, Row A, Seat Five. An afternoon concert at the Cow Palace featuring The Kinks. As Sam Curtis ushered The Kinks onstage, I took one photo of Ray, Pete and Dave. The Kinks wouldn't be performing, he announced, as they hadn't been paid by the very promoter who not only provided my bus ride to SF but also served post-concert burgers and fries to all onboard. Had my hunger been satisfied by food bought with money that should have gone to pay The Kinks? Had I unknowingly contributed to their three-year blacklisting?

Years later, I showed Dave that photo. He referred to Pete as 'Crutch'. The way he'd brushed his hair back then, Dave thought he looked like Paul Samwell-Smith, The Yardbirds' bassist. I smiled, happy to contribute memories.

Thank you, Kinks, for rocking my innocent heart.

Alain Noslier – Saint-Malo, Brittany, France

In the summer of 1965, I was 14 years old and living in the old farmhouse where I was born in a small village called Le Petit-Paramé, a few miles from the town of Saint-Malo in Brittany, France.

My holiday friend, Nadine, was a year or two older than me. Nadine ... where do I start in explaining my meeting with a mermaid? At least that's how she appears to me, 58 years later: A young girl with a golden-brown skin like honey, light brown eyes and a beautiful smile to take your breath away. The first time I met Nadine in the village square, I fell in love with her.

She came from Tours in the Loire Valley, and she was staying with her parents in a small, rented apartment by the village square, half a mile from where I lived. The asphalted square – surrounded by houses, a grocery shop and a bar – was where everyone met for parties and games. Before cars were invented, it could have been covered with grass like a village green.

During July 1965, I met Nadine virtually every day in this square to talk about music, the city lights and swimming on the nearby beach. I was attracted to popular British music since I'd heard The Beatles singing 'She Loves You' only a few months before. Apart from this, what could adolescent dreams be made of if not meeting the opposite sex and reaching nirvana by kissing a girl on her lips for the first time?

At 8 pm on 26 July, the evening before she had to go back home with her parents, I had a rendezvous with Nadine planned in the village square. I looked forward to that moment all day while building castles in the sand, hoping and dreaming I would experience my first French kiss with her. But that fateful evening, she was nowhere to be seen. I waited for what seemed an eternity, but she never turned up.

The next morning, I asked people she knew if they had seen her the previous evening. Someone said she had gone to a friend's house to see a television program called *Discorama*, featuring an English band called The Kinks playing live in Paris. I had never heard of this band before. Living in the countryside, I wasn't up to date with British bands. I pondered why such a friendly and beautiful girl like Nadine stood me up and preferred to see 'a bunch of clowns called The Kinks gesticulating on stage with their dishevelled long hair.' It was such a massive and hurtful disappointment. The higher the expectation, the lower and bigger the fall. But like Ray Davies often sings, there's always a bit of blue sky or sun piercing through the clouds and the rain.

In September of that year, I fell ill and was stuck in bed for two weeks. I listened to the radio to keep boredom at bay, and a song they kept playing was 'A Well-Respected Man' by a band called The Kinks. I don't remember whether I made the link with Nadine standing me up, but I recall Ray's sad tone in the song's delivery. It reflected my own melancholy, particularly in the lines: 'And he plays at stocks and shares/And he goes to the regatta/He adores the girl next door/'cause he's dying to get at her'. Call it coincidence, but why would Ray's phrasing of those lines resonate with me? In those days, my English was far from fluent, but the mood fitted my sadness. I must have listened to that song hundreds of times, and always those lines would hit me.

A week later, seeing my infatuation with that Kinks song, my elder brother offered me my first-ever record: The *Well-Respected Man* EP. What a moment of gold that was! If Nadine had been there, I would have shared my first kiss with love and harmony. I never looked back, becoming a fervent Kinks fan and even moving to London for 17 years (from 1972 to 1989), hoping that one day I would run into The Kinks and my hero, Ray Davies, to tell him this story and all that The Kinks gave to me. I finally met him in 2018 at The Clissold Arms in Fortis Green – a treasured moment to complete the circle.

I never met Nadine again. But if you see her one day, please tell her what she inspired. For a glass that started half-empty, I am glad to say it ended up more than full to the brim.

Olga Ruocco – Langdon Hills, Basildon, Essex, UK

Ah, 16-year-old me, a Kinks fan for just over a year, when I got the surprise of my young life – and I've lived long enough to tell the tale!

Friday, 12 November 1965: I was lounging about, just home from school, looking a right scruff in my school uniform and planning to have a long, warm bath. There was a sound of a motor scooter in the street outside, and this insane thought popped into my head: 'That's one of The Kinks coming to visit me, ha ha.' I told myself not to be so stupid, but seconds later, there was a ring at the doorbell. Mum opened the door and a voice asked, 'Miss Ruscco?' I went into the hall, and there was Pete Quaife standing there! I'm not given to screaming, but I could have screamed. I just went, 'My God, it's

Pete!' Can you just imagine? A member of my favourite group is in my house! Flesh and blood, he's standing there! He'd sent me a very funny letter the month before (which is dearly treasured to this day), and he wanted to follow this up with a visit to a fan who lived just down the road from Muswell Hill.

I'm consulting my Kinks diary for that day. Considering my stupefaction, I must have been staring very hard at him to remember what he was wearing: a greenish cap, an anorak, a red polo-necked jumper, black trousers, black socks, grey suede boots and a college scarf. He'd come out in the freezing weather just to see me! Mum made him a cup of instant coffee that he dubbed 'Nescaff' and he proceeded to tell us about his visit to the US, his new scooter, the *Kinks Kontroversy* album, the next single ('Till The End Of The Day'), filming, girls, flying and his family.

I think he stayed talking to us for about an hour and a half. He was just so easy to get along with, and within minutes, it all seemed perfectly natural for him to be sitting in our front room, chatting away about everything. He told us that he'd bought a new scooter. His old one had been stolen, but he managed to get it back. Then it got smashed up by some bloke who claimed diplomatic immunity, which didn't go down well with Pete.

He and Dave Davies had been watching *Top Of The Pops,* and there was a gorgeous girl with dark hair in the audience. Both he and Dave rushed off to drive to the BBC Television Centre to find her but got there 20 minutes too late. She was nowhere to be seen.

Pete explained that when you sang in the studio, you had to put a finger in your ear so that you could hear yourself, and he didn't understand how people could scream when they were recording as a group of blokes stared down at you from the control room.

Pete and Mick Avory stayed with a family when they were in the US, and he decided to make an English Sunday dinner for them: roast beef and all the trimmings. He was looking for an Oxo cube to make the gravy, but the family had no idea what that was, and they brought out a can of gravy instead. They all trotted off to the local supermarket and found the Oxo cubes in an obscure corner of the shop.

Apparently, he heard a German girl on the plane saying that English chaps had no manners. That made him angry, and he invited her out to dinner, then a nightclub and a taxi back to her home. He really put on the works and did everything he could for her. At the end of the evening, he kissed her hand and she said, 'By the way, I've changed my mind. The English do have manners.'

He explained that he loved flying, and while in Iceland, he took a plane to the new volcano and filmed it erupting. When they landed in Saigon, the plane went 'bomp bomp' and his spine nearly went through the back of his head. He liked the VC10 as it was a vertical take-off, and the ground seemed to drop away. There was a dear little old lady who wanted to go to the toilet, and both were in use. Innocently, he said, 'Why don't you try that one?', pointing to the aircraft door. She tried it, and the stewardess came along and gave him a right telling off. The old woman still thought it was a toilet!

He told us that his brother, Dave, was like Steve Marriott of The Small Faces but a bit shorter. He tried very hard to be a Mod, and all the girls liked him. I would meet Dave a while later when Pete invited me to Sunday tea, but that's another story!

Alfons Wagener – Aalten, The Netherlands

In 1965, my mother visited her sister, who told her that her son was a member of an organisation that had contracted The Kinks for a gig in Winterswijk, Holland. My mother decided to buy two tickets for my brother and me.

On the day of the concert (Sunday, 21 November), the weather was very bad, so The Kinks arrived very late in Winterswijk. My brother and I decided to stay, even though the last bus to our hometown left at midnight. The Kinks arrived after that, and we saw a very good but short performance. We were very pleased. After the show, we had to walk to our house – a trip of 12 kilometres – but the show was worth it.

After seeing this performance, I became a Kinks fan. I bought all the LPs and CDs, and also the solo albums from Ray Davies. I listen every day to their music.

Joe Wood – Somerset, Massachusetts, US

The Kinks arrived in America in 1964 or '65. I was ten years old. I had three siblings in their teens, all avid radio listeners: two girls and a boy. I am sure I first heard 'You Really Got Me' and 'All Day And All Of The Night' from and with them.

My Kinks conversion began in 1965-66 when I was 11 or 12 and had to be in bed at 9 pm. I was lucky enough to have a small battery-operated transistor radio – AM only. (Remember them?) I would go to bed and put my radio under my pillow, so my parents could not hear it.

In those days (and probably still true), AM radio, under certain conditions, would create great 'skips' in broadcasting. Being outside of Boston, I would often lose the signal listening to WMEX and WBZ. I would lie there trying to fine-tune the dial and, to my great surprise, tune in to radio stations from Buffalo, New York or Montreal that sounded clearer than my local stations.

This is where I first heard The Kinks that I came to love and follow. I am not sure which was the first song I heard this way. It may have been 'Dedicated Follower Of Fashion', 'A Well-Respected Man' or 'Sunny Afternoon'. I like to think it was 'Sunny Afternoon' because that is one of my favourite songs. I could not wait to share this information with my friends. It wasn't until years later that they caught on to the greatness of The Kinks when *Muswell Hillbillies* finally got their attention.

I have only seen The Kinks live once. It was in Providence, Rhode Island, in the foggy years of 1970-72. I do not recall which year or which venue it was. It was a great show, my friends tell me, still.

George Mariner – Philadelphia, Pennsylvania, US
My love for The Kinks goes back to 1965. When my dad was driving, he would always let me listen to my favourite radio station – WIBG in Philadelphia. One day, 'All Day And All Of The Night' came on. It was The Kinks' new record. 'Dad, turn this up!' There had never been a song that sounded like this. Wow! I've never looked back. I've been a fan ever since. Greatest band ever!

1967
Phil Richards – Banbury, Oxfordshire, UK
The first concert by The Kinks that I attended was in 1967 in Rugby, Warwickshire, UK. In his book *All Day And All Of The Night: Day-By-Day Concerts, Recording And Broadcasts 1961-1996*, Kinks historian Doug Hinman records it as the Ben Memorial Ballroom on Friday 16 June – all details I had forgotten.

I do remember that the hall was absolutely packed, and most of the audience were standing. Some way into the concert, a power cut threw us all into darkness and, of course, cut off all the instruments and sound system. I don't think much time passed before we were up and running again, and the lads continued as if nothing had happened!

It was my first sight of the live Kinks, and everything that came later seemed to fit into that pattern of accidental disorganisation that we've been used to ever since.

David Titterton – Tamworth, Staffordshire, UK
In the autumn of 1967, I met a girl at a youth club in Erdington, Birmingham. The night I met her, the band playing was The Idle Race, Jeff Lynne's band. Yes, *the* Jeff Lynne. The girl's name was Linda, and she was into Motown and the dance music of the time. I was already into The Kinks. I played a lot of football and trained, and we drifted apart in the spring of 1968. Football took up too much of my time. When The Kinks released their single, 'Days', I thought of Linda every time I heard it. I could not get her or the song out of my head.

One warm summer evening, I went with a friend to a local funfair, and by chance, Linda was there that same night. We saw each other and started talking. One of the things Linda told me was that she had bought the 'Days' single because it reminded her of me. I will always believe that song helped us get back together, and we have never been apart since. We now live in a house which we named Shangri-la. Thank you for the days, Ray.

Harald Gottsknecht – Hildesheim, Germany
My first contact with The Kinks happened in 1967 when my cousin told me that he wanted to record 'Waterloo Sunset' with his reel-to-reel tape recorder while it played on the 'Hit Parade' from a local radio station. The song was brand-new and high in the German charts.

My second contact was the broadcast of 'Plastic Man' and 'King Kong' by Deutscher Soldatensender 935 KHz. This was a very strange radio station because it was near the Iron Curtain border at the Harz Mountains in East Germany and managed by the German Democratic Republic to broadcast fake news to the armed forces of the Federal Republic of West Germany.

After hearing these songs, my curiosity was awakened. A few weeks later, I talked with guys at school who were two or three years older than me, and they sold me a French copy of *Face To Face* in a German-lettered sleeve. It began a lifetime love of one of the greatest bands of all time.

Unfortunately, I hated live music for years because the songs sounded too different and, in my opinion, unbearable. It took a very long time (and a Mike Oldfield gig) to discover the charm of different arrangements of well-known songs. So it's a shame that I witnessed live Kinks experiences only twice: 8 December 1987, with Marquee Moon, and 6 December 1993, with Katrina & The Waves – both in Hannover at the Capitol, a former cinema.

Since then, I've tried to see every Ray or Dave Davies gig possible, and each of them was a highlight in my musical life. The final one (so far) was seeing Ray at the Guildhall in Southampton in 2012. I went with a colleague, Dirk Zörner, who is a die-hard Kiss fan. We'd previously travelled to the Netherlands to see Snowy White in Weert and Ray Davies in Amsterdam. For the journey to Southampton, we created T-shirts with a caricature of Ray on the front and a 'God Save The Kinks' logo and 'From Hannover To Southampton' on the back.

The guy who did the warmup for Ray (I think it was a local street musician) took a photo onstage to prove he played for such a big audience. You can see us almost in the middle of the photo as two 'bright persons' amid the crowd.

1968
Ruud Kerstiens – Nieuwegein, The Netherlands

Some events in your life leave an indelible impression. For me, it was the first performance of The Kinks that I attended.

I was 17 years old, still living at home and listening to the pirate radio stations that broadcast from the North Sea – Radio Veronica, Radio Noordzee, Radio London and many more. That's how I first heard the music that I continue to love to this day, most importantly, The Kinks. Ever since 'You Really Got Me' (my very first 7" single) pleasantly surprised my eardrums in 1964, I have been a continuous and diehard fan of the band and the solo careers of Ray and Dave Davies.

On 19 May 1968, Cliff Richard topped the Dutch charts with 'Congratulations' and The Kinks stormed into the charts with 'Wonderboy'. I was fortunate to have a ticket for my very first Kinks concert in a café hall in Vlagtwedde, a village in northeast Holland. As soon as the hall doors opened, I looked for a nice spot close to the stage. The supporting act, a then-popular Dutch band called The Scandals, played longer than planned because … where were The Kinks? They seemed to have lost track of time.

The bar was doing good business, and I got into conversation with a guy called Dieter, a German concert-goer. He turned out to be a novice journalist from the magazine *Musik Parade* who was sent to Vlagtwedde to write a review of the show. He knew little about The Kinks apart from a few hits, and his editors told him to ask his questions mainly to Ray Davies, who – he heard – wrote and sang most of the band's songs. But which of the four Kinks was Ray Davies? He didn't know.

The Kinks arrived around 10:30 pm. To prevent Dieter from asking his questions for Ray to the wrong band member, he asked me to accompany him to the dressing room. All the doors opened for us, all the security people gave friendly nods, and before we knew it, we were face-to-face with The Kinks. What a moment! I quickly checked my Kodak Instamatic camera for this special photo opportunity.

It was busy in the small dressing room because not only The Kinks were there but also people from the record company and others who were part of the tour. I saw Ray and Dave Davies and Pete Quaife and … where was Mick? Pete told me with a big smile that Mick went to the toilet immediately upon arrival, but 'he will be here in a minute.'

Dieter put his questions to Ray. I tried to get photos – in their travel clothes – and autographs of all four band members. The highlight was the photo with Dave, on which I got his autograph. Security began to see that I was not in the dressing room as a professional journalist but as a fan. A broad-shouldered security guard asked me to leave as quickly as possible, and he tolerated no contradiction. My dressing room adventure was over, and I went quickly back to the hall.

The Kinks appeared on stage around 11:15 pm. From that moment on, the audience – just like at every other concert at that time – went completely crazy. We'd all been waiting for this. As soon as Ray Davies took his place behind the microphone, he was no longer the shy artist I encountered earlier in the dressing room. Ray and The Kinks went all out to 'give the people what they want' with all the hits from 1964 to 1968 at full volume, including 'Wonderboy' and Dave's solo hit, 'Death Of A Clown'. Later that year, the *Village Green Preservation Society* album would be released, but no previews of that masterpiece were shared that evening.

The rest of the audience and I enjoyed every moment, singing along to all the songs at the top of our lungs. Just before midnight, The Kinks called it quits after about half an hour and a short 'encore'. Ray, Dave, Pete and Mick left the spotlights of Vlagtwedde; the sound equipment was turned off, the hall lights came on and we let the crowd take us to the exit and into the cooling, somewhat chilly night. We hardly noticed it because of the adrenaline that still flowed through our veins.

After this memorable evening in 1968, I saw The Kinks and Ray and Dave live many more times, and I thoroughly enjoyed it just as many times, but that evening in Vlagtwedde was never to be forgotten.

Michael Hanratty – Ferryhill County, Durham, UK

On 20 October 1968, The Kinks were on a cabaret tour in the UK and appeared at The Top Hat in Spennymoor County, Durham. I was 16 years old, and with my scrapbooks and albums, I walked three miles to Spennymoor, hoping for some autographs.

The Kinks arrived in a Ford Zephyr but were rushed into The Top Hat, and I failed to get any autographs. The following night, they did the same and rushed in, but a roadie named Roger saw me and we started chatting. He asked me to help carry Mick Avory's drums up an outer set of steps into the club.

I was invited into their dressing room, where they signed my albums and scrapbooks. I remember telling Dave that my friends liked The Small Faces, and Dave said he liked them, too. To my amazement, Roger the roadie asked me to sit with him behind the amps, and when Ray asked him to turn a knob on the amp, I got to do it. Roger told me they used to spray crazy foam at each other for fun.

After the show, Ray was arguing with – I think – the manager of The Top Hat, and Ray kept chanting to him, 'WE DON'T WANT TO HEAR IT!' I wonder what that was all about. After The Top Hat, they had to go to Stockton Fiesta to perform. I kept asking the guys about the release of the *Village Green Preservation Society*, and they said there was a disagreement with Pye about adding 'Days' to the album.

I will never forget my experience meeting them, with thanks to Roger the roadie. The Top Hat is still there (not as a nightclub), but my memories will never fade. I'm 71 years old now, but I still love them to bits.

The 1970s

After a slide in popularity at the close of the 1960s, The Kinks started the new decade with one of the biggest singles of their career. 'Lola', the story of a naïve man's encounter with the titular transvestite, hit number two in the UK and number nine in the US while also charting high worldwide. It marked the first recording for new band member John Gosling (nicknamed 'The Baptist' because of his long hair and stoic mien) on keyboards.

'Lola' buoyed sales for the next album, 1970's *Lola Versus Powerman And The Moneygoround, Part One,* a not-so-subtle takedown of the music business. The renewed success also allowed the band to negotiate a new contract with RCA Records, which funded the construction of their own North London studio, Konk, and gave them more creative and managerial control.

The first RCA album, 1971's *Muswell Hillbillies*, proved to be a pioneering country-rock album. Coming just three years after The Byrds' *Sweetheart Of The Rodeo*, the record gave a British working-class twist to the emerging genre. A brass section, The Mike Cotton Sound, joined The Kinks in the studio on *Muswell Hillbillies* and then on tour until the late 1970s.

Everybody's In Show-Biz, a double album, featured half studio recordings and half live recordings from New York City's Carnegie Hall. Intended as the soundtrack for a tour film exploring the trials of road life, the film never materialised. Many of the new tunes – apart from the heartfelt 'Celluloid Heroes' and 'Sitting In My Hotel', both favourites among fans – showed a campier, more theatrical style that continued over the next few years with the rock operas *Preservation Act 1* and *Act 2, Soap Opera* and *Schoolboys In Disgrace*. More members joined the touring lineup, including female backup singers.

With the US touring ban lifted, The Kinks slowly rebuilt their fanbase there through relentless touring around the country, especially at colleges and smaller to mid-sized venues. Sales of the rock-opera albums, however, did not reflect these efforts, with *Schoolboys* scoring highest at number 45 on the *Billboard* chart. The British record-buying public showed no interest.

When RCA dropped the band after *Schoolboys*, they signed to the newly formed Arista Records in 1976. Ray Davies, encouraged by Arista founder Clive Davis, reinvented The Kinks for the arena-rock era, ending the rock-opera format and returning to songs independent of any connecting storyline. The gamble paid off: *Sleepwalker* heralded the new deal with a number 21 showing on the *Billboard* chart. The next album, *Misfits*, did not score as highly, but follow-up *Low Budget* proved to be the most popular Kinks record ever in America, hitting number 11.

Bassist John Dalton left the band during the *Sleepwalker* sessions and was replaced by Andy Pyle – then Andy and keyboardist John Gosling left together after *Misfits*. Ex-Argent bassist Jim Rodford assumed bass duties, with Gordon Edwards (formerly of The Pretty Things) on keys, but Ian

Gibbons took over from Gordon by the end of the 1970s. Ian (barring a gap from 1989 to 1993) and Jim would be part of the lineup until the final Kinks shows in 1996.

For many American fans (those who love the rock opera shows or their hard-rocking turn with Arista), these were the glory years.

Albums by The Kinks: *Lola Versus Powerman And The Moneygoround, Part One* (1970), *Percy* (1971), *Muswell Hillbillies* (1971), *Everybody's In Show-Biz* (1972), *Preservation Act 1* (1973), *Preservation Act 2* (1974), *Soap Opera* (1975), *Schoolboys In Disgrace* (1975), *Sleepwalker* (1977), *Misfits* (1978), *Low Budget* (1979)

1970
Dave Moore – Minneapolis, Minnesota, US

When The Beatles hit, I was a mid-teen stuck in 1964 small-town Iowa, where the drug store sold only non-rock LPs. When my dad went to bigger cities, I gave him lists of 45s to bring back (songs I'd heard on top 40 radio from Des Moines), leading to discussions about wasting my allowance, but he did it. As an aspiring writer, I was always partial to sharp lyrics.

Among the 45s was 'You Really Got Me' and I spent hours playing Dave's monster guitar break on my tennis racket. I continued to gather every single they released until 'A Well-Respected Man' knocked my socks off and etched The Kinks solidly in my teenage heart. The B-sides got almost as much play on my little portable record player. My last single purchase was 'Sunny Afternoon' – imagine my delight when I flipped it over to find 'I'm Not Like Everybody Else', which was an arrow to my heart.

Time and Bob Dylan happened. In the fall of 1967, I went off to college. I still listened to the top 40 stations, but The Kinks had faded. I didn't know about the band's ban, and I was entranced by the 'white blues' wave. By 1969, I shifted to college in Wisconsin (where Cream and Frank Zappa played at Homecoming), got married and found myself on a tight budget that didn't allow music purchases. I also no longer listened to the radio much. Mostly, I played albums I owned, though I had no Kinks.

Then, in 1970, on an infrequent trip to the local shopping centre, I browsed the cutout bin at Zayre's. There were a few BYG Records samplers of British blues that I've never seen anywhere since and, *at 29 cents apiece*, the first EIGHT US Kinks albums in mono. I took those babies home!

Fulfilled, I spent many happy hours immersed. I forget how I acquired discarded record club copies of *Village Green* and *Arthur*, but their attention to story enthralled the lyric-lover in me, not to mention they rocked. Enthusing about them to a classmate who DJed at the campus radio station, he said, 'No one wants to play this', and he presented me with their copy of *Lola Versus Powerman*!

That ushered me into Kinks heaven, where I have lived ever since.

1971
Lynn Killam – Almond, North Carolina, US

I was 15 years old in March 1971. With my best friend, I walked into New York's Philharmonic Hall and entered a new world. Blue smoke swirled around our heads, and loud, thumping music played as everyone found their seats. I had no idea what awaited us. It was my first of 40 Kinks concerts.

When Ray came onstage, my life changed. I'd always loved Kinks music – y'know, top 40 and all that. But I never really understood them until that night unfolded. The band were, how should I say … *loose* that night. Sloppy, even. But exciting, intoxicating and fascinating. Ray was obviously on something, but I didn't care. He was sex on legs for me that night. He was bawdy and campy, and Dave was playing slashing guitar behind him. Mick was driving the beat, as he always did. Those were the three I watched the most, although John Dalton and John Gosling were quietly dignified during the craziness. Well, up until Ray fell into the speakers, that is. Then everything took a turn. Everyone in the first two rows, including me, jumped onstage and watched Ray get carried away as roadies tried unsuccessfully to push everyone off. Cacophonous yelling and feedback replaced the music until, somehow, we all got back into our seats and Ray came back onstage. He resumed the set as if nothing untoward had happened. We sang along, we stood up and cheered, we laughed and I believe I cried at the end. I never wanted it to end. I bet that was the last rock concert held at the Philharmonic.

Several Carnegie Hall concerts were next (they hadn't heard what happened at the Philharmonic?), then the Schaefer Music Festival in Central Park, the Felt Forum shows and a few at colleges in New Jersey and New York. I somehow talked my way backstage at their Fordham University and Rider College shows (I don't remember how, but I'm certain tears were involved), and the Capitol Theater sets were incredible. Once, a couple of my girlfriends and I went to Philadelphia and got a hotel room to see them at the Spectrum, and I have such fond memories of seeing them at the Beacon Theater and the Palladium.

The *Preservation* shows and then *Soap Opera* were not everyone's favourite, but I loved them simply because I loved The Kinks so much. And I adored Ray. He could do no wrong with me. A musical genius and a born performer – he was why I kept coming back.

The Kinks enriched my New York City years. I think they saved me from an alcoholic parent and the stressors of late adolescence. The music, which I played repeatedly until the vinyl was potato-chip thin, was complex yet straightforward. Ray's voice could change from a soft lilt to a roar as he switched up musical styles on every song. The Kinks' music was original and magical, and so were their concerts. I saw David Bowie, Queen, The Tubes, Bruce Springsteen, The Pretenders, Elvis Costello, Lou Reed, Rockpile and many more, but The Kinks were completely different from anyone else. I continued to follow them through NYC, Philadelphia and New Jersey. Then I moved to Houston, and it was harder to see them. The last time I saw them was in February 1985 at the Music Hall – not the best venue for them, and something seemed different. When I left that last show, I felt crestfallen and somehow knew it would be my last.

Forty was a good number. It was enough, and it left me with memories I'll treasure for the rest of my days. I thank my lucky stars for The Kinks, their music and the endorphins that they gave me every time I went to hear them play.

Bernard de Gioanni – Nice, France

I have known The Kinks since 1965, and I became a real fan in 1967 with albums like *Face To Face* and *Something Else*. Later, the greater the quality of their albums (like *Village Green Preservation Society* and *Arthur*), the more they were underrated and forgotten, especially in France. I was very upset about that. I had to do something. In the summer of 1971, I put an advertisement in a French music magazine called *Salut les copains*, looking for other Kinks fans. A young Dutch couple on holiday in Paris bought it at random, and back in Holland, the guy gave it to his young sister (who was 18 years old). She found my advertisement and wrote to me. I invited her the next Christmas, and a love story was born.

We met several times with difficulty (Nice is 1,500 kilometres from Amsterdam!), and we finally began to live together in mid-1973. Later, we married and had two children, and we are still together today. Thanks, Ray!

De Gioanni founded and ran the Kinks French Konnektion fan club from 1977 to 1984, producing the fanzine *Kuppa Kinks*.

Robert Shulman – Houston, Texas, US

I went to a Kinks concert on Staten Island in New York in November 1971. Yes were the opening act. It was my first time seeing The Kinks; I had tickets for a show a few years earlier, but it was cancelled when they were barred from performing in the US.

In those days, security wasn't so tight, and I was able to sneak backstage. I was in awe of being that close to the band that had been my favourite for so long. I remember being struck by how tall Ray was. I told him that listening to their records and seeing them on TV made them seem kind of unreal and that meeting him somehow made my connection to them palpable. He thanked me in a soft, shy voice. When I ran into Dave, I asked him about his solo album, which seemed to have been talked about for ages – he groaned and dashed away. Mick and John Dalton seemed like down-to-earth guys.

I had brought blank sheet music and got their autographs. Eventually, I came down off the cloud …

1972
Kate Ratigan – Greensboro, North Carolina, US
I'm 65 and consider myself a lifelong fan of The Kinks. Anyone who knows me knows *that* about me! It started when I was very young because my older brother, Kevin, was an avid music fan and had discovered British Invasion bands. He was particularly fond of The Rolling Stones but collected everything, including The Kinks. One day, I heard 'Sunny Afternoon' for the first time and just loved it! I drove Kevin insane, asking him to play it over and over. Of course, he did because I was so little and cute back then!

The fire was ignited, but it really exploded in 1972 when *Everybody's In Show-Biz* came out. Kevin played 'Celluloid Heroes' for me, and I was officially in love with our Kinks. While friends had photos of David Cassidy on their walls, I had photos of Ray Davies! Kevin took me to see them at Westbury Music Fair in 1995, which turned out to be one of their last shows in America.

In 2001, Kevin was killed in a car accident. Our family was devastated, naturally, but I still think of all the fond and funny Kinks-related memories I have with my favourite sibling. (Sorry, Gail and Mike!) Kevin left behind over 1,000 albums. His widow was not willing to part with a single one because she'd planned to sell them all together. My sister Gail and I managed to steal a few, among them *The Great Lost Kinks Album* and two others I did not have! I thank my beloved bro and friend, Kevin Ratigan, for introducing me to The Kinks.

1973
Paula Diemer – Marlborough, Massachusetts, US
In 1973, I was 15 and a high school student in suburban Providence, Rhode Island. Listening to WBRU, the Brown University radio station, I heard 'Celluloid Heroes' for the first time. 'You can see all the stars as you walk along Hollywood Boulevard …' Of course, I'd heard The Kinks on the radio in earlier years, but I fell in love with this song. I started collecting the albums – scouring cutout bins to add to my collection – and attending the gigs. At the time, Providence seemed to be on an at least annual tour schedule, so I got to a fair number of gigs from 1974 to 1980, mostly in theatre-style settings, though the venues got bigger toward the end.

In 1981, I was 22 and just out of college. I moved to Los Angeles with my partner, who was offered a transfer within his company. I found a job with offices that just happened to be on Hollywood Boulevard, so I saw all those stars every day as I walked along Hollywood Boulevard. Never did get to any LA gigs, though – I wasn't as tempted during the arena era, much to my regret now.

1974
Bill Cannon – Palatine, Illinois, US
My introduction to The Kinks led to 50 years of loving the band as well as Ray and Dave Davies's solo shows and releases – CDs, concerts and books.

I knew The Kinks had done 'Lola' but never sought out anything about them – I just liked hearing 'Lola' on the radio. In my first year of college at Western Illinois University, I met a fellow freshman named John Costello, who is, to this day, one of my best friends. He knew I was into music, which at that time was Elton John, The Rolling Stones and The Beatles, with some Harry Nilsson and Randy Newman thrown in. He told me he had a great cassette of songs by The Kinks, and he was positive I would love it.

Once John put on the tape, the music hit me like a bolt of lightning. It started with 'You Really Got Me', 'All Day And All Of The Night', 'Tired Of Waiting', 'A Well-Respected Man' – each of which I said, 'That's The Kinks?!' He then played 'Sunny Afternoon', 'Victoria' and others. When the tape was done, I was on a mission to hear more Kinks – which I did. I started with *The Kink Kronikles*, found *The Great Lost Kinks Album* in a cutout bin and had a guy on my floor play me the whole *Lola Versus Powerman And The Moneygoround* album – again, I was floored. I thought these guys should be as big as The Beatles and The Rolling Stones.

The next year, I bought a ticket to see The Kinks in Chicago. Cheap Trick opened the show and were excellent – the crowd loved them. Next, Little Feat played and raised the show to another level – again, just great. Finally, The Kinks came out and played the old hits and did the *Schoolboys In Disgrace* album, which was the topper!

I eventually bought all their albums and had the pleasure of meeting and talking for some time to Dave. I mentioned how I thought *Schoolboys* started their resurrection and how his guitar playing on that album and going forward was simply the best. In addition to loving The Kinks, I also embraced some of Ray's common themes – be true to yourself, don't compromise in life, screw the corporation and the crooked politicians.

Finally, I took a friend to see Ray at the Chicago theatre. He is a big Queen fan and was somewhat doubting how good the show would be. His reaction: 'I didn't know The Kinks wrote all those great songs, and their lyrics tell great stories.'

Thanks to The Kinks for a lifetime of joy.

Wendy S. Duke – Akron, Ohio, US

1965: My first Kinks encounter. A friend taught me how to pick out the chorus of 'A Well-Respected Man' on my guitar. I thought it was a fun song with an interesting premise. (I did not buy the record.)

1972: I was preparing to graduate from college with a theatre degree. Between classes, we would go to Mark's apartment, smoke some dope and play 'Celluloid Heroes' over and over again. I had lost touch with The Kinks, but the lyrics to this song coloured my perception of what it means to act and perform on stage for an audience. (I loved the album but did not buy it.)

1974: Now a college grad and stumbling around trying to find a paying gig, I landed a job as an FCC log-checker and PSA writer for WCUE AM/FM. What a time to be plunged into the world of rock 'n' roll! As soon as I was hired, I knew I wanted to be an on-air voice, but I had so little knowledge of the music. Fortunately, the guys on the FM side of the dial were more than happy to help! Late at night, after the suits went home for the day, the community bong came out, presided over by the chief engineer. At the time, FM radio was still an experiment, and nobody on the business side thought it could ever make money. Yet, a short distance north, WMMS was starting to make waves with progressive underground programming.

At WCUE, the AM side represented the plutocracy and proudly programmed commercials for banks and automobile dealerships. The AM jocks were stars who made local appearances and raked in extra cash. They played top 40 hits from a playlist that was strictly determined by the AM program director.

On the FM side, all the jocks were paid minimum wage ($1.60 per hour in Ohio in 1974). The FM program director was a big, warm bear of a man named John Griffin. His job was to program the music and promote the station – with a budget of no money! All the jocks loved him because he seemed to have no rules about what anyone could play and for how long. Segue competitions were a thing! As one tune ended, another tune would begin on another turntable, and the trick was to find intros and outros from different songs that magically merged in that segue moment.

John was a big Kinks fan. One memorable day, he asked me if I'd listened to The Kinks' *Preservation* albums yet. He said, 'Wendy, this is rock 'n' roll theatre! You will love it!' He had seen the concert tours for both *Acts 1* and *2*. He whipped out *Act 1*, put it on the turntable and played it on air in its entirety, followed by *Act 2*. As I mentioned, in those miraculous days, nobody paid attention to what the FM side was doing!

While we listened to the albums, John gave me his running commentary about the plot, the characters and how The Kinks presented the show. I was pulled in by the story of the rise of Mr. Flash while his rival, Mr. Black, plotted his takeover. It had elements of a medieval morality play, complete with a chorus of Do-Gooders denouncing sex and sin. By the end, the story takes a dangerous sci-fi twist with the entrance of the Mad Scientist, who turns everyone into artificial beings. Artificial intelligence before it became a thing! The entire *Preservation* saga continues to live before its time.

I could go on and on about this work, but I don't need to because I wrote and presented a paper on 'The Theatrical Elements Of The Kinks' *Preservation Acts 1 & 2*' at a pop culture symposium decades after John Griffin shared his passion for The Kinks with me. Yes, dear readers, I did buy *Preservation Acts 1 & 2*, as well as every Kinks album prior and everything since!

Sadly, WCUE FM became a threat to the AM side, and all of us on the FM side were fired for being too radical. I never saw my FM radio pals again. I keep hoping they are out there somewhere – around the dial.

1975
Julie Evelsizer – Tuscaloosa, Alabama, US
I had been a Kinks fanatic since 1969 or 1970. I longed to see them live, but since I lived in Alabama, they never played anywhere near me. And in those days before the internet, information was hard to come by. I don't remember how I found out The Kinks would be playing in Memphis, Tennessee. It was probably an ad in *Billboard*, which I scanned each week in search of news about my idols.

It was 1975, I was 19 and I couldn't drive. I also had no money, but I did have a friend who wanted to see The Kinks as badly as I did. She, in turn, had a friend who had another friend in Corinth, Mississippi, who she wanted to visit. We must have had nearly $40 among us. We caught a ride as far as Corinth with the lady who had a friend there, and we bought bus tickets the rest of the way to Memphis.

We arranged to stay at the shabby motel across from the bus station and walked to the venue. It was a small place down near the river. Members of the Children of God cult hung around outside, and when we told them the story of our trip from Tuscaloosa, they said they could use such devotion in their group!

The concert was *A Soap Opera*. We walked right in and took seats in the 11th row. It was tremendous. Full of awe and excitement, we walked out into the late night, stopping to recall which way we needed to turn back to the motel.

A big gold car pulled up with three golden women inside. 'Y'all working girls?' the driver asked, and I realised I had stopped in front of a porn outlet! 'No, ma'am', I said and quickly chose the right path out of there.

As expected, we could not sleep the rest of the night, and with sore throats and hands from all the screaming and clapping, we made our connection back to Corinth and Tuscaloosa. It was a night never to be forgotten.

Around The Dial With … Martin Hutchinson
My memories of The Kinks go back to the start when my sister, who was a teenager, used to listen to Radios Luxembourg and Caroline. The music seeped into my young consciousness. I was five years old when 'You Really Got Me' came out, and I liked it even then. In fact, I liked all the singles.

Fast-forward to the mid-1970s, when 18-year-old me bought all three 'Golden Hour' compilation albums and realised that there was more to the band than just the singles, so I began to collect the back catalogue. I was helped when, in 1979, the Mod revival resulted in the release of all the original Pye albums, and from *Misfits* onwards, I bought each new album as it came out.

The lyrics and musicality of The Kinks really took hold of me, as each album had something special. I was especially fond of the mid-1970s albums, from *Soap Opera* to *Low Budget*, and my fandom eventually resulted in me writing my first book for Sonicbond.

I was lucky enough to see the band in concert twice, in 1980 and 1981. They played Blackburn in 1994 and I was horrified when I didn't find out until 2004!

The stage production of *Sunny Afternoon* is another highlight of my Kinks fandom – especially when, during the curtain call, Ray Davies came onto the stage.

Great music and great memories.

Hutchinson is the author of *The Kinks: Every Album Every Song*, part of the 'On Track' series from Sonicbond Publishing. He lives in Bolton, UK.

1976
Stefan Gies – Wipperfürth, Germany

I'd been a Kinks fan for 11 years but had never seen my 'heroes' live. I missed the concerts during the 1960s, and in the 1970s, I only found out about the Hamburg concert in March 1976. I bought tickets early on, and although it was supposed to start at 8 pm, I started driving my old Beetle from Cologne to Hamburg around 7 am. I was full of anticipation and, of course, well equipped with a camera and an Uher Report (a portable stereo tape recorder).

Arriving in Hamburg, I heard Kinks tunes on the car radio, followed by an interview with Ray Davies. I stopped at the next taxi rank and asked where to find the NDR broadcasting station. Unfortunately, when I finally got there, The Kinks were no longer there, but I met Christian Wagner, the director of the legendary Rockpalast, who wanted to sign them on his television show (which he finally did five years later). It turned out that he was also a big Kinks fan, and he gave me a tip to try the Hotel des Congress Centrums, where The Kinks were staying.

I drove to the hotel and sat in the lobby. After about 20 minutes, my breath caught and I broke out in a sweat – I couldn't believe my eyes! Mick Avory came down the stairs and went to the reception desk. A few minutes later, Dave and Ray Davies, John Dalton and John Gosling followed. I thought: 'It's now or never.'

I summoned all my courage and went to see Mick and Dave. A friend took photos and ran the Uher Report while I babbled some nonsense in my schoolboy English. Mick took the time to talk to me and was very friendly (as were the others). When I asked Dave for a beer, he said that, unfortunately, he had to go to the rehearsal, but I could accompany them if I wanted to.

It was amazing! Suddenly, I was on stage with The Kinks, recording everything and taking photos while they did their soundcheck. At that time, there were 11 people on stage – in addition to the five already mentioned, Nick Newell, John Beecham, Alan Holmes, Pam Travis, Shirlie Roden and Debi Doss were present.

After about two hours, the soundcheck was over and I was the happiest person on earth, even though the real highlight – the concert – hadn't even started yet. The show featured a few classics at the beginning and the *Schoolboys In Disgrace* show afterwards, but it couldn't top my afternoon experience. Ray Davies delivered an almost-perfect performance (complete with a beer can on his head during 'Alcohol') and appeared as the 'Headmaster' with the well-known mask. Dave was as good as ever on lead guitar and played fantastic solos. The announcements explaining the *Schoolboys* story were made in German by one of the singers.

Thanks to the Uher Report, the soundcheck and my crude interview attempts have been preserved for posterity.

1977

Kent Crawford – Horse Heaven Hills, Washington, US

When The Kinks released the *Sleepwalker* LP, the song 'Sleepwalker' was all over the radio in Los Angeles on KMET 94.7. My childhood friend Bill and I used to stay up all night, and we would get into people's cars and steal things. One of the things that I acquired besides a wind-up alarm clock, loose change and terrible cassette tapes was an eight-track of *Sleepwalker*. As a juvenile delinquent sneaking around, just like in the lyrics, I related so well to the song.

As we know, Ray and Dave Davies are brothers, and my brother and I grew up during this rock 'n' roll era. Every time a Kinks song came blasting out of the radio, we kind of looked at each other and said, 'Oh yes – those guys!' It's a memory that I will treasure always.

Ray and Dave have influenced me spiritually and musically, and thinking about it reminds me of a time that we all just can't get back.

Jay Kunst – Woodside, New York, US

My first 'unrealised' exposure to The Kinks was in 1977 at the age of 14 while at summer camp. Our counsellor would wake us up every day with 'Good Morning' by The Beatles and a second song about a character who crept around at night. I never got the title of that song, but I loved it. Once camp was over, I never heard it again.

Fast-forward to the summer of 1979 and out comes *Low Budget*, with several songs getting airtime on FM radio. I bought the album and enjoyed it so much that I decided to look for others by this 'new group' that weren't so new as it turned out. As I flipped through albums (of which there are many), the greatest hits one made me realise how many of their songs I'd heard on the radio, like 'You Really Got Me', 'All Day And All Of The Night' and 'Tired Of Waiting'.

Undecided about what album to get next, a guy recommended *Schoolboys In Disgrace*, so I went with that. I also picked out a second album, *Sleepwalker*, because the cover looked cool. After listening to *Schoolboys* first, I proceeded to drop the needle on *Sleepwalker*. My brain sprang into alert as the third song and its strumming intro let me know I'd heard this before. I couldn't believe my ears – I found the song my counsellor had played for us daily for two weeks almost two years earlier.

My life changed as I bought every Kinks album. Numerous concerts followed, from 1980 at Nassau Coliseum to 1981 at Madison Square Garden up to 1993 in Jones Beach, New York. Just a small story of my knighting into the Kinkdom.

Konrad Kauczor – Berlin, Germany

I was born in 1953 in Cottbus in the German Democratic Republic, known to most people as East Germany. It was socialist from its founding in 1949 to the fall of the Berlin Wall in 1989, which meant that the government carried out unchallenged autocracy and was 'democratic' every four years with an almost 100% voter turnout and an almost 100% election victory for the Socialist Unity Party of Germany.

Life in the GDR was structured: kindergarten to school, then training and the army and finally a job. Anyone who became more informed soon hit ideological limits. Western radio and television were not banned, but they were not supposed to leave the private sphere. It was almost impossible to get hold of Western records, magazines or books. People of the same age communicated more openly, but you never knew whether conversations or activities were reported to state security.

The first time my two older brothers, my younger sister and I heard 'Dedicated Follower Of Fashion' was on a borrowed tape recorder around 1966, when I was 13 years old. When we had an old tube radio, my brothers listened to the few Western stations that broadcast hit parades, such as Radio Luxemburg, on the shortwave. In addition to other beat group songs, we learnt Kinks songs such as 'Dandy', 'Sunny Afternoon', 'Dead End Street', 'Autumn Almanac', 'Mr. Pleasant', 'Days' and 'Wonderboy'. When ´Plastic Man' aired on the Beat Club Radio Bremen, I knew this was my band.

From then on, I collected everything about The Kinks: magazine articles, pictures, songs and lyrics. To listen to music independently, I purchased a tape recorder and exchanged recordings. Over the years, the recording conditions improved: the FM stereo reception in Cottbus was poor, especially when cars with non-spark-suppressed radios rattled through. That was in the 1970s when I was about 20 years old. A high point in my being a fan was when I received a Ray Davies photo with an autograph in 1971, which the London editorial team of *Bravo* magazine got for me and sent to Poland. I picked it up from relatives and smuggled it home sewn into my anorak.

The wish became more urgent to travel to West Germany after retirement at the age of 65 to experience a Kinks concert – if the band still existed by then! Of course, the lack of basic democratic rights – such as freedom of travel, demonstration, information and speech – left me dissatisfied.

At the beginning of 1976, when I was 22 years old, something had to happen. Without much detail, I'll mention a few keywords here: attempted escape entering the border area, capture and pre-trial detention for five months. The court verdict: a 20-month prison sentence. After five months, I was ransomed by the West German government. Now, I was much closer to my goal. It was wonderful to listen to Kinks songs and LPs that had been unknown to me.

In the fall of 1977, the time had come. As part of an educational leave to London, I used my free time to visit the *Bravo* editorial office in London and got the address of Konk Studios with the condition that I should not try to go inside. From the Kinks song 'Nine To Five', I figured out the studio's closing time.

On 23 September, I saw from a distance first John Gosling, then Dave Davies and finally Ray Davies walking out of the studio to a car. I couldn't be held back anymore – I had to talk to him and ask for a photo. When he asked where I came from, I said 'from Germany.' 'Thank you very much' was all I got in reply. The fact that coincidences happened in such a way that enabled my lifelong dream to come true still makes me happy!

I saw my first Kinks concert a year later, on 16 October 1978, in West Berlin. Today, at age 70, I have seen the Kinks in concert 21 times, Ray Davies 18 times and Kast Off Kinks ten times.

I rarely tell my story because most people can't understand it – except for Kinks fans!

Chuck Harter – Los Angeles, California, US

In the 1970s, I lived in Alexandria, Virginia, which is right next to Washington, D.C. The Kinks usually played at least once a year in the area, and I always went because I was a huge fan and had all their records.

On 10 December 1977, The Kinks played at the Capitol Centre Stadium, opening for Hall & Oates. Near the end of The Kinks' set, I realised they probably would be leaving the arena. I ran around to the back and found only four people waiting by a bus. After a while, the band came out and I yelled greetings to each member. Mick Avory was last. I ran up to him and said he was one of my favourite drummers and that I wanted to shake his hand. He thanked me and shook my hand. I asked him where they were going, and he said to the Holiday Inn.

As the bus drove away, I realised I knew where it was and drove there to maybe hang out with the band. I ended up in a small lounge where a polyester-clad four-piece band and a female singer were performing. They were doing mostly Olivia Newton-John and Linda Ronstadt covers. There were five or six people in the lounge with a bartender, and nobody seemed interested in the music.

After half an hour, I was about to leave when Mick, keyboardist John Gosling and bassist Andy Pyle walked in. I jumped up and told them I had just seen the show, and Mick invited me to sit with them! Mick and John went to the bar and returned with two bottles of Heineken in each hand. They put two down in front of me. At this point in my life, at 24, I hadn't drunk much alcohol, but that was about to change. They each raised a bottle, clinked them with mine and downed the beer in one swallow. Not wanting to be left out, I did the same. I very quickly became tipsy and began babbling to them how much I liked the *Sleepwalker* album and their music in general. Looking back, they were remarkably kind to an enthusiastic fan. After a few more beers, I was getting plastered while they seemed hardly affected.

At this point, the lounge band announced a ten-minute break. Gosling went up to one of them and said he was with a band. Could they do a few numbers on the group's instruments? They reluctantly agreed. As the three went up, Mick asked me if I played guitar. I said I did, and he invited me to join them on the small stage!

Gosling sat down behind a keyboard and announced, "Little Queenie' in A.' He sang it, and we did another oldie that I can't remember. None of the patrons or the bartender paid any attention to us. By now, the members of the lounge group were making motions for us to stop. I went to the mic and announced, 'We'd like to do our first hit', then went into the opening chords of 'You Really Got Me'. They fell in, and there I was, singing 'You Really Got Me', drunk out of my mind while backed by The Kinks to an unresponsive audience of a few.

I was a good rhythm guitar player but couldn't play lead at all. When it was time for the solo, I dropped to my knees like Dave used to, turned up the guitar and played the worst shredding solo! The three Kinks were laughing so hard they almost stopped playing, but somehow, we got through to the end of the song.

As we came off the stage, my adrenalin was in overdrive. They all shook my hand and got some more beers. Soon, I began seeing double and knew I should leave, so I told them thanks for the jam. They hugged me and, while laughing, said it was great to play with me!

Somehow, I made it home without crashing the car. The next day, while nursing a colossal hangover, I reflected that I sang The Kinks' first hit … while backed by them … to an audience that couldn't have cared less. Glory! God save The Kinks!

Around The Dial With … Vincent Palmer

I was 13 when 'You Really Got Me' was released. Since my teens were punctuated by the amazingly aggressive riffs of The Kinks, when the time came in 1977 to start my own band, Bijou, one of our very first compositions – 'C'Est Un Animal' (in its 45 rpm version) – was inevitably inspired by the riff of 'All Day And All Of The Night'. But so that it was no more than a hint, I limited myself to the first two chords. Since the melody had nothing to do with it, I was worried that this nod to my favourite band wouldn't be too discreet, but I was reassured and pleased when I heard Suzi Quatro's rendition of 'Tired Of Waiting' starting with the same riff with the same beat, the same breath and almost the same sound. Fortunately, Suzi's cover came out the following year, otherwise, you'd have thought I copied it. That said, I still wonder if it wasn't the opposite ... but thanks to Suzi for making my initial intention more consistent.

In 1993, during the promo tour for the last Kinks studio album, *Phobia*, I was invited to back Ray Davies for a showcase on a barge on the Seine River in Paris. Very exciting! Flattered and happy to finally meet the man who had rocked my youth, I took time to sharpen up a few of his famous riffs before putting on my most perfect dark suit with a brand-new white shirt. To my surprise, when we met on the barge that afternoon, he was dressed very casually, to say the least.

This difference in appearance between us must have irritated him, this and the fact I dared to ask him – because of the lack of rehearsal – if he wouldn't mind adding 'Louie Louie' to the setlist, which he promptly rejected. At the end of the showcase – why I really should have avoided the damn suit – he introduced me as 'Eric Clapton'! Big bursts of laughter in the audience followed.

Palmer was the founding guitarist for the French power trio Bijou and later became a music critic. He is based in Paris, France.

1978
Jim Terrinoni – Oswego, New York, US
Although I saw The Kinks in concert about eight times, my most memorable Kinks moment was at the historical Landmark Theater in Syracuse, New York, in 1978. It was after President Richard Nixon became famous for his arms up in a 'V' formation, with each hand making the 'V' peace symbol. As the crowd waited for the concert to start, Ray – dressed in a Nixon mask – came on stage right with his arms and fingers up in the 'V' formation. He circled to stage left and exited. Then, he re-entered as Ray and – *BLAM!* – right into the opening number. Ray being the entertainer extraordinaire and because of the time frame (after Vietnam and Cambodia), it was one of the funniest ways to get the audience's attention.

1979
Rick Ulrich – Florence, Oregon, US
After a Portland show on the *Low Budget* tour in August 1979, my girlfriend and I went to the Hilton and called Ray from the lobby. I told him that I had a screen, a 16mm projector and a film I had made using 'Holiday Romance' as the soundtrack. This was a couple of years before MTV, of course. He came to the lobby and met us, then sent us with his bodyguard to his room to set up. We were left alone with a case of Heineken beer, which we were told to enjoy while we waited for Ray. He came in and had a private showing of my film. He said he had the same kind of projector (B&H). He also claimed to really

enjoy the film, and on the way out, stopped at the bar and bought us a bottle of French Champagne. I still have the bottle.

Years later, I spoke with him after a *Storyteller* show, and he still remembered the film. He signed my 1966 white Fender, and I gave him an 8x10 photo I had taken of Dave at the *Low Budget* show.

Greg Rutford – Jackson, Wyoming, US

Tucson, Arizona, on 7 September 1979 – the concert that in many ways changed my life. A co-worker asked me if I'd like to see The Kinks that night. Sure, I knew a few of their hit songs, but that was about it.

There was no opening act. You could feel the energy building as the house lights went down and out came The Kinks. Some bands just have that stage presence, and Ray and Dave had the crowd in their hands. I remember many things about that show: Ray changing outfits every few songs, the mask he wore for one number and him sitting on a chair playing acoustic guitar for 'Lola'. What a performer! Just incredible music all night long. Dave's guitar was awesome, showcasing great solos and thundering rhythms.

I became a lifelong Kinks fan that night. After the show, I went to the record store and bought four Kinks albums. I would have bought more, but that was all the cash I had on me. I have turned many others onto The Kinks since that day. I saw them another four times and have seen Ray solo. I love The Kinks and the music they have made – thank you!

Brigitte Jeffs – Epsom, Surrey, UK

Growing up in Germany in the late 1960s, when I was about eight years old, I started to notice and like The Kinks a lot when hearing their songs on the radio. I bought some of their albums with my pocket money and hoped to see them live. Unfortunately, they never played in or near my hometown, Stuttgart, and so I had to wait until I passed my driving test.

Finally, on 5 November 1979, they were playing in Mannheim, about 140 kilometres away. I drove there straight after work and arrived in time for the concert. I don't remember much of it, only that I was in heaven and there was a ripped sheet at the back of the stage!

After the concert, I waited at the stage entrance. After a while, Ray, Dave and Ian Gibbons came out and signed a piece of paper for me. I was starstruck and unable to talk, and I could only mumble 'thank you.' I still remember Ray coming out, clutching a bottle of champagne, and Dave asking me to go back to his hotel with him, but he was quickly ushered into a waiting car. He then wound the window down and repeated the invitation just as the car drove off. A memorable evening.

I had a photo that I took of Ray blown up and I hung it in my bedroom. Little did I know that I would decide to move to England nine years later (mainly because of Ray's songs), eventually meeting all the members of the band (except Pete Quaife) and becoming friends with some of them.

The Kinks eventually played in Stuttgart on 21 December 1994, and so did Dave Davies solo on 7 October 2001, but I lived in England then. When we saw Ray in March 2023, I mentioned to him that The Kinks played in my hometown; he remembered and immediately said, 'Mercedes.'

Around The Dial With … Glen Burtnik

I was almost ten years old, already well into pop music and paying close attention to everything and anything that my two teenage brothers had to say regarding the culture and style of the time. By this point, the so-called British Invasion was in full swing. Inspired by Ringo Starr, I took drum lessons (thanks, Mom) and I was pretty much glued to the two competing New York City radio stations playing the hits of the day: WABC and WMCA. That's where I must have first heard the raucous 'You Really Got Me' single. I took note, but I was a little more into The Beatles and The Dave Clark Five to be sure about this wild sound.

Television was also a resource back then. There wasn't much rock 'n' roll to view in the early 1960s. There was *The Ed Sullivan Show* and *American Bandstand*, each having maybe two songs lip-synced by bands with current hits, but the rest of these shows were much less interesting to me. Then came *Shindig!*. Before the British Invasion took over boomer culture, there was a popular folk music movement. When polite acts like the Kingston Trio, Trini Lopez and Peter Paul & Mary were hot, there was a successful TV show called *Hootenanny*, which catered to the current folk artists. However, after The Beatles, the folk revival fizzled out, *Hootenanny*'s ratings tanked and *Shindig!* was created as a show to replace it. I'll never forget seeing The Kinks singing their explosive, rowdy rock on *Shindig!* It was electrifying, and it left an impression on me I still can't shake loose.

About 15 years later, in 1979, I was a professional musician with the Broadway show *Beatlemania* and a member of the staff invited me out to the White Horse Tavern (famous for being where the poet Dylan Thomas drank himself to death). She told me Ray Davies might join us, so I grabbed my friend Tony and we drove into Greenwich Village from New Jersey. Sure enough, Ray showed up with The Kinks' drummer Mick Avory and bassist Jim Rodford. We sat at a round table, drinking and politely talking. Ray struck me as a gentleman, and Mick was rougher around the edges but friendly. I was young and too much of a fanboy to really have much of an intelligent heart-to-heart with Ray (beyond some Chris Farley-esque 'You're great!').

It was decided we'd go to the Mudd Club (I think it was) afterwards and it was there that I had a better conversation with Avory and Rodford. I got to describe the effect of seeing The Kinks play 'You Really Got Me' on *Shindig!* and how moving it was. (I also shared with Rodford how much I loved Argent because he was the bassist with that band as well.) Ray had silently disappeared by then, as rock gods do.

Burtnik is a singer, songwriter, bassist and multi-instrumentalist known for his work with Styx and Electric Light Orchestra and his portrayal of Paul McCartney in the Broadway production of *Beatlemania*. He performs as Lefty Weekling in The Weeklings, a band based in Asbury Park, New Jersey, that celebrates the music of The Beatles and other bands of the 1960s. They contributed their recording of 'Lola' to the 2023 tribute album *Jem Records Celebrates Ray Davies*.

The 1980s

As the decade opened, The Kinks' arena-rock era reached its pinnacle with a live double album, *One For The Road* (number 14), and studio follow-up *Give The People What They Want* (number 15). As if to remind listeners where the songs originated, *One For The Road* included several Kinks classics that had recently been recorded by others, such as 'David Watts' (The Jam), 'Stop Your Sobbing' (The Pretenders), 'The Hard Way' (The Knack), 'You Really Got Me' (Van Halen) and 'Where Have All The Good Times Gone' (David Bowie, later also covered by Van Halen). The albums did not chart in the UK.

The relentless touring during this period led to sellout concerts, not just in the US and UK but also in Australia and Japan, including a 1981 show at New York City's iconic Madison Square Garden and an appearance at the 1982 US Festival in California for a crowd of more than 200,000 people.

The band's improved commercial standing allowed Dave Davies to fulfil his long-held ambition to release his own solo albums. The most successful, 1980's *AFL1-3603*, peaked at number 42 on the *Billboard* charts, with some songs reflecting his interests in Eastern religions and mysticism.

The Kinks' final big hit, 'Come Dancing', was a throwback to Ray Davies' British pop roots, complete with a big-band horn section that felt quite different from the guitar-driven rock of the Arista era. Inspired by his sisters' dubious dates in the 1950s, Ray waxed nostalgic about the local Palais, where all the cool kids used to dance the night away. The UK single in November 1982 didn't garner much attention, and a US release followed in April 1983.

US sales skyrocketed when the music video, directed by Julian Temple, got heavy rotation on the fledgling MTV network. 'Come Dancing' hit number six – the highest-charting US single of the band's career, tying with 'Tired Of Waiting For You' from 1965. UK listeners took notice, boosted by a re-released single in July and an appearance on *Top Of The Pops* in September, the band's first since 1972. It peaked at number 12 on the UK singles chart. 'Come Dancing' lifted *State Of Confusion* to number 12; its second single, the gentler ballad 'Don't Forget To Dance', hit number 29.

Between touring obligations, Ray wrote and directed a film, *Return To Waterloo*, for the UK's Channel 4. The story – told almost entirely in song – followed the fantasies of a traveller (Kenneth Colley) taking the train to London from the suburbs. Members of The Kinks, minus Dave, recorded the soundtrack and several songs appeared on the next Kinks release, *Word Of Mouth*. Unfortunately, the momentum from 'Come Dancing' had slowed, and the album reached only number 57 on the US charts. Dave's fan-favourite track, 'Living On A Thin Line', later appeared on the television show *The Sopranos* (and nearly became the theme tune).

Between *Return To Waterloo* and *Word Of Mouth*, founding drummer Mick Avory left the group but stayed in the Kinks organisation to manage Konk Studios. His replacement was ex-Argent percussionist Bob Henrit, but Mick occasionally contributed to future recordings.

In 1986, The Kinks signed with MCA Records in the US and London Records in the UK. The three records released during this period – *Think Visual* (number 81 on the *Billboard* charts), *Live: The Road* (number 110) and *UK Jive* (number 122) – featured many good (often great) tunes but underperformed sales-wise as hair metal and pop ruled the end of the decade. After *UK Jive*, keyboardist Ian Gibbons left the band and was replaced by Mark Haley.

For many American fans, these were the glory years (especially the first half of the decade). The British record-buying public loved 'Come Dancing' and ignored the rest.

Albums by The Kinks: *One For The Road* (1980), *Give The People What They Want* (1981), *State Of Confusion* (1983), *Word Of Mouth* (1984), *Think Visual* (1986), *Live: The Road* (1988), *UK Jive* (1989)
Album by Ray Davies: *Return To Waterloo* (1985)
Albums by Dave Davies: *AFL1-3603* (1980), *Glamour* (1981), *Chosen People* (1983)

1980
Around The Dial With … Ron Sexsmith

In 1979, I was 15 years old and in the car with my dad when 'All Day And All Of The Night' came on the radio. I'd never heard it before, and it was one of those rare moments in life when you become aware that you've found something you didn't know you were missing. I'm sure it had the same effect on me as it did on anyone hearing it for the first time in 1965.

I went to Sam The Record Man the very next day and purchased an album called *Golden Hour Of The Kinks*, and my life hasn't been the same since. Up until that point, I had dreams of maybe being a singer for some band, but this record made me want to be a songwriter. The obsession had begun, and whenever I had enough money from mowing lawns, I'd buy whatever Kinks record I needed.

Around this time, they came out with a double live album called *One For The Road*, and on one popular radio station, they had a contest where they gave away records each week to whoever could imitate whatever band was being featured. On this particular week, it was The Kinks' *One For The Road* album, so I called up and managed to get on the show. After singing a few bars of 'Lola' (in a fake British accent), I won the album!

In 1980, some friends from high school told me that The Kinks were coming to the Buffalo Auditorium on 17 October. Buffalo was directly over the border from where I lived in Canada, about half an hour's drive. We all went down to Sam The Record Man and purchased tickets for what we were sure would be an amazing concert. This was all happening at a time in my life when going to concerts meant finding some kind of booze or drugs to enhance the experience. Back then, you didn't need a passport to cross the border, so we'd all pile in someone's car and head down – usually stoned out of our minds. On this particular night, we all dropped acid, but it hadn't taken effect yet.

We suffered through the opening act, and I started noticing that the acid was kicking in. At one point, I even saw someone in a giant chicken costume walking around and selling something. Before we knew it, the concert had begun with brother Dave Davies walking out and playing a cool instrumental version of 'You Really Got Me', followed by a punky version of 'The Hard Way'. I realised that they were basically playing the same set as on the *One For The Road* live album, but it didn't matter – I was entranced.

Later in the show, they performed 'Celluloid Heroes'. It came to that part where Ray sings, 'Success walks hand in hand with failure down the Hollywood Boulevard', and I had a sort of profound moment. It felt as though Ray had sung it directly to me or that he had somehow singled me out in that huge crowd. Everything seemed like it was in slow motion. His hands literally reached out to me with this important message. As we drove home from the concert, it was all I could think about.

Years later, in 2011, I performed at the Meltdown festival in London, which was curated by Ray Davies himself. I told him this very story before the show, and he seemed to get a kick out of it. Halfway through the show, he came out and joined the band and me for a version of 'Misfits' – but before we sang it, he asked me to tell the audience what I had told him backstage. (Somewhere, there's a clip of this on YouTube!)

From the age of 15 to this current day, The Kinks have been my favourite band. I never gave up on them. Their music changed my life to the point where it's fully in my DNA. I saw them on numerous occasions when they were still performing, but that first night in 1980 will always stand out to me as one of the truly great shows I've been fortunate enough to witness.

Sexsmith is a three-time Juno Award-winning singer-songwriter from Ontario, Canada. He has released 18 albums and contributed a cover of 'This Is Where I Belong' to the 2002 tribute album *This Is Where I Belong – The Songs Of Ray Davies & The Kinks*.

Adrian Long – Somerset, UK

I have been a Kinks fan since August 1964 when I heard 'You Really Got Me' on my dad's transistor radio on the beach at a little place called Charmouth in Dorset. After hearing that seminal riff and the sound of the guitar, I was hooked.

Fast-forward to 1980, I had been married for three years and we took our first holiday abroad together – a coach trip to Ostende for a week. Travelling home, I spotted a poster advertising a Kinks concert at Friars in Aylesbury the following week. We both worked in a shoe factory for C&J Clark Ltd., making (mostly) kids' shoes, and we had another week off because the factory was shut down to do maintenance.

As soon as I could, I phoned the venue, but they said all the tickets had gone. I was absolutely gutted! It must have sounded down the phone because she told me to ring again later to talk to a bloke called Dave Stopps, who was the organiser of the gig, as he ran a 'special list' that he compiled. I was desperate to drive up there from Ilminster in Somerset in our Moggy Minor, so I rang again without any conviction that I would even get to talk to him! The phone rang, and the bloke who answered was Mr. Stopps! He had been out with the band for a pre-gig meal. I asked him about his 'special' list – he clocked my very broad *zummerzet* accent and complimented my super-keen pleading! So, beyond my dreams, we were added to the precious parchment, and we were to pay on the night. (Not *that* generous, then!)

We set out in our gunmetal grey 1963 Moggy, arriving in good time to suss out somewhere to stay the night. We went to the tourist info centre in Aylesbury and got a bed-and-breakfast opposite a cemetery that was so big it could have been Flanders. It was run by an ex-army sergeant. Everything was spotless, and he cooked a fantastic full breakfast in the morning. I must have looked a sight to him with beyond-shoulder-length red hair! But he was an okay guy and ran a great place.

We went up to town for a wander for a couple of hours to get closer to the doors opening at the venue. I remember buying an album in the record shop but cannot remember what it was. (My 39-year-old son has all my vinyl now!)

When we got to Friars, there was a waist-high barricade around the front that meant you could not get past it without showing your ticket to the bouncer guys. Bollocks – we never had any! I didn't do anything spectacular to get past him other than keep saying that if he came with us, he could see our names on the 'holy list'. Eventually, he relented, and we got to the box office. We gave the girl our names, coughed up the dough and in we went like a dream. I had never been there before, and there was a bar, too!

Suffice it to say, the boys were brilliant, and I had one hell of a headache when I awoke the next day to look out the bedroom window on the vast field of the dead.

Around The Dial With ... Keith Topping

We have an old 1960s reel-to-reel tape recorder in our house which contains, amongst other things, a three-year-old me in the summer of 1967 singing 'Autumn Almanac' with my brother and one of his friends. *Really* badly. This author first actually owned a Kinks record in 1970 (the 'Apeman' single, for those taking notes). But this story isn't about those things. This is about Jacob's Club biscuits.

For the uninitiated (and all Americans), Club was (and still is) a range of (very nice) chocolate-covered biscuits made, initially, by the Irish company Jacob's of Dublin that became hugely popular in Britain in the 1970s. They did very famous TV adverts featuring an annoying earworm of a jingle ('If you like a lot of chocolate on your biscuit/join our club!'). They produced several varieties, including their bestseller, the Orange Club, which is still available to this day. The ones I used to particularly enjoy as a youngling were the milk chocolate brand (in a red wrapper) and, particularly, the dark chocolate version (with a golf ball on the green wrapper for some obscure reason related, no doubt, to a golf club pun). Sadly, Jacob's stopped making those sometime around 1983 when Nabisco acquired the company. A twenty-four-carat tragedy.

Marginally related to this nonsense about chocolate, I have in my record collection *Called To The Bar*. This was a 16-song vinyl compilation LP from 1980 featuring some great 1960s and 1970s pop tunes – mostly from CBS Records, whom Jacob's had obviously done a deal with, probably because, at that time, they were using a cover of The Beach Boys' 'Barbara Ann' on their latest TV advert. It featured a stereotypical Teddy Boy in the dock of a court singing 'Bar-bar-bah, bar-bar-bah-ba-Club' after the usher had shouted 'Prisoner at the bar ...' A reasonably flattering bit of artwork of the actors involved is featured on the LP's cover. One merely collected about 12 Club biscuit wrappers (any variety would do), sent them along with 50 pence to cover postage and you got the LP by post.

There were a fine bunch of songs on the LP, and it may well have been the first place I ever heard top tunes like The Honeycombs' epic 'Have I The Right?' or The Love Affair's sublime 'An Everlasting Love'. It was certainly where I first owned Fleetwood Mac's 'Albatross' or Thunderclap Newman's 'Something In The Air'. In fact, apart from a thoroughly puke-inducing Dr. Hook dirge on side two, I believe I still have just about everything on the LP somewhere in my CD collection. Even the one by Tina Charles.

Nevertheless, to cut this overly long-and-winding story shorter, the reason why *Called To The Bar* still holds a major (and, by major, I mean brigadier-general) place in my heart was that it was the first record I ever owned to feature 'Waterloo Sunset'; then, and now, one of my favourite songs of all time. It marks – along with a purchase soon afterwards of a second-hand copy of *Something Else* so I could hear what their (retrospective) cover of The Jam's 'David Watts' sounded like (ahem) – the beginning of a 50-year love affair between me and The Kinks.

We'll never know if Terry and Julie had any Clubs back at their gaff where they felt safe and sound (or, indeed, if any could be found on 'Dead End Street'). Nevertheless, I'd like to express my sincerest hope that at least a portion of the royalties accrued from the 12 Club biscuits I purchased to acquire *Called To The Bar* ended up in Ray Davies' pocket (minus whatever income tax was due, obviously). To save him from the squeeze. Hopefully, too, for licencing the song to Jacob's, Ray got himself a lifetime supply of Clubs. He certainly seemed to gain a bit of weight during the early 1980s; perhaps now, we know why.

Topping is an author, journalist and broadcaster who has written more than 40 books on *Doctor Who, Buffy The Vampire Slayer, The X-Files*, The Beatles, The Clash, and more. He lives in Newcastle upon Tyne, UK.

1981
Paul Englund – Windermere, Florida, US
I was 12 years old and just getting into music. I was riding in the car back from the beach with my friend John, and I heard the last minute or so of 'Lola'. It stuck in my head, and I knew I needed to hear that song again.

I jumped on my bike and rode to the Broward Mall in Plantation, Florida, where I headed to Record Town. I found The Kinks section among the other cassettes (because I was in the cassette phase of my music collecting) and started looking. I had no idea what I was looking for or what the song's real name was. There was not a huge selection of tapes, so I grabbed the first one. *Give The People What They Want* was the name on it. I looked at the songs and saw a song called 'Yo-Yo'. I sang it in my head and thought: 'Is that the song I heard? Lola? Yo-Yo?'

I bought the tape and rushed home to listen. I quickly learned that 'Lola' and 'Yo-Yo' are not the same song, but that album began my lifetime love of The Kinks. To this day – 25,000 pieces of music later – it is still one of my favourite albums.

That's how a stupid kid who didn't know what he was looking for discovered one of the greatest bands in history!

Hisao Handa – Tokyo, Japan
The first time I heard The Kinks was 'You Really Got Me' on an oldies show on the radio when I was 15 or 16 years old. That characteristic guitar riff left an impression! A few years later, an older music-loving friend lent me a best-of vinyl album, so I recorded it on a cassette tape, discovered other great songs and fell in love with the band.

In the early 1980s, Kinks LPs were hard to come by in Japan, so cassette tapes were important. There were only five titles available: *Sleepwalker*, *Misfits*, *Low Budget*, *One For The Road* and *Give The People What They Want*. However, thanks to the band's first performance in Japan in 1982, the masterpiece albums of the Pye era were re-released and available in Japan. Albums from the RCA era were difficult to obtain, but I managed to get two as imports at a record store in Akihabara, Tokyo: *Soap Opera* and the compilation *Celluloid Heroes*. I really liked these albums and listened to them over and over.

Unfortunately, I couldn't go to their performance in Japan in 1982, but it was recorded and broadcast on FM radio. I recorded it on a cassette and treated it with care. Eventually, it was released as a bootleg record.

Fast-forward to 1993. Just when I thought they wouldn't come to Japan anymore, The Kinks decided to tour here for the *Phobia* album! Thanks to the kindness of a friend who arranged for the ticket, I was lucky enough to get a coloured piece of paper signed by Ray and Dave Davies, and I also got one for my younger brother, who went to the concert with me. I was grateful. The performance was amazing – I have never experienced a better concert than this one. Another visit to Japan, which I thought would never happen, actually did in 1995! What's more, in December of that year, Ray also did a solo performance.

The Kinks were relatively underrated in Japan and not very popular, but there was a bit of a Kinks boom going on at that time. As if to prove this, an album from the RCA era that had been out of print for a long time was re-released in Japan. I've been able to obtain and listen to all of The Kinks' original albums since the 1980s in real time. There are no bad Kinks albums! It's a shame there have been no original albums from them since then.

When I visited the UK several times in the past, I went to places connected to The Kinks: Muswell Hill, the Archway Tavern, Highgate, Hampstead Heath and Waterloo Station. I'd love to go there again, but I don't think I can do it anymore.

1982
Steven Burgess – Ridgeway, Virginia, US
On the morning of 13 January 1982, with 16 inches of snow on the ground, my wife and I left Martinsville, Virginia, with two friends to travel to Hampton, Virginia, to see The Kinks play at Hampton Roads Coliseum.

The driving was not too bad, given the conditions. After about 25 miles, the engine started overheating due to the radiator hose rubbing against a fan pulley. We made it to an auto parts store in Danville, Virginia, purchased a universal hose, installed it and headed off for Hampton. Unfortunately, the underlying issue was an incorrectly installed engine, and it continued causing problems for the rest of the trip. It was cold, with no heat or defroster because of the leaky hose, and the windshield was coated with ice. Driving was difficult. What should have been a four-and-a-half-hour drive ended up taking about ten hours, with the car getting worse by the mile. By the time we got to the James River Bridge, which is 4.4 miles long and leads into the Hampton area, we decided to head to the show and worry about the car later.

By the time we got to our seats, we got to hear only the final three songs. Fortunately, the band played three encores of three songs each, and we got to hear 12 songs in total. The band and Ray had the audience in their hands and put on a fantastic show. The applause between the second and third encores was deafening. Suddenly, all the house lights came on and the crowd's enthusiasm crashed. Just as quickly, the lights went dimmed and the band came out for their final encore.

After the show, we found an all-night auto repair shop, got the hose problem fixed and headed home. I remembered that The Kinks would be playing in Charlotte, North Carolina, four days later, so we decided to go. On the afternoon of 17 January 1982, the four of us headed off for Charlotte. The temperature was frigid, with forecasts for lows near zero degrees Fahrenheit. We made it to the Charlotte Coliseum on time and got to see the whole concert. The band were fantastic, but the crowd weren't. It never approached the intensity of the one we saw just four days earlier. The end of the show was the same as in Hampton, except when the lights came on after the second encore, the audience just assumed the show was over and got up and left. Needless to say, the band did not come out for a third time. It's amazing how the audience can affect a performance.

On the way home, about an hour into a two-hour drive, we started getting low on gas. Our driver said we'd be okay and we'd get to a station before we ran out. We didn't. As his punishment, we voted that he would be the one to get some gas. As late as it was, with little traffic, it probably took an hour or so for him to return. With the temperature near zero, we thought we'd freeze to death. We finally got gassed up and headed home. About ten miles away from our destination, we ran out of gas again and had to call our driver's father to come bring us some gas. It was probably 4 am.

Though it was hard at the time, with all the auto and weather problems we faced, now they are just good memories of an opportunity to see The Kinks in two cities within four days.

June Terrell – Memphis, Tennessee, US

After winning a trip to Hawaii, I returned home on the same day The Kinks played at the Auditorium North Hall in Memphis on 14 June 1982. I took a purse for the two shirts I purchased before the show, and my ticket stub was also in it. During the concert, someone stole my purse. I went looking for it when the hall was empty. A roadie threw some backstage passes, and a girl caught all three. I begged her to give me one, and she finally did. I put it on and proceeded backstage. I went straight to Ray, who was signing autographs for a few people. I told him, 'Thank you for all the enjoyment your music has brought me all of these years.' He gave me a very sincere thank you. He seemed genuinely touched.

We went to The Peabody Hotel, where the band were staying, and I ran into Mick going into the lobby. He stopped and talked to my brother and me, asking us questions about how the concert sounded. I asked the hotel clerk if Ray Davies was staying there, and she said band members were booked under anonymous names. She suggested that if I wanted to leave a note for him, she would make sure he received it.

The next morning, I returned to the hotel with my camera and waited for them to leave. While I was outside, I took a photo of Mick getting into the limo. Then I saw Dave and his wife and children, and I started to take photos of them. Dave started yelling at me and acted as if he was going to charge over to stop me. I went back into the hotel. Then, I saw Ray as he made his way across the lobby to leave. I went outside, and there was a guy from a radio station wanting to interview him. I asked Ray if I could take his photo, and he agreed. I then asked if he could step into the sun so I would have better lighting. He asked me if my last name was Terrell. I answered yes, and he told me he received the note I left him at the front desk. I freaked out and could not believe he remembered my last name. The radio guy asked if I wanted him to take a photo of Ray and me. I was so in awe of Ray talking to us and me taking his photo that it went right over my head. I have regretted it ever since. I felt like I was invading his privacy by taking his photo and bothering him while he was trying to leave. Ray was so down-to-earth both times I encountered him.

The Kinks did not play any concerts (that I know of) near Memphis after that show in 1982. I still listen to them and love them to this day!

Marianne Spellman – Kirkland, Washington, US

12 June 1978 was a momentous day for me: my very first Kinks concert and my very first time using a 35-millimeter camera. The next year, I met someone who knew them, and she invited me to meet the band. At 17 and from a very small town, I never dreamt this would be possible. I very awkwardly met Ray, and I later showed him my photos from the year before. He thought they were very good. Wow! The next year, after I graduated from high school, I spent most of the next four years seeing and photographing as many Kinks shows as I could, with Ray or Big Bob Suzynski kindly and amazingly providing access for me. Later, many of the photos were published in several Kinks projects. What a dream come true!

On 19 June 1982, at the old JFK Stadium in Philadelphia, I attended a concert featuring The Kinks, Foreigner, Joan Jett, Huey Lewis and The News and Loverboy. I avoided the massive crowd on that brutally humid day until The Kinks' set. I'd never been to a show that large, never mind tried to photograph one. The stage was so high and there were so many sweaty, drunken bodies already pressed up against it that I wasn't sure what I was going to do. But to be able to take pictures of my beloved band in the daytime without the challenges of indoor stage lighting? I was going to figure it out.

I made my way to the front, by this time experienced in rock 'n' roll crowd navigation. But it was not good. I am short, and the stage felt like it was 30 feet high. I had no sightline, and moving back into the crowd was equally useless. I spotted a plastic milk crate under the stage, asked security for it, rammed it against the foot of the stage to steady it, and climbed up just as the band took the stage. It made me another foot taller, but the ground wasn't level.

The crowd pushed forward as the opening music played and BOOM! – I fell off the carton, flat on my butt into the crowd, protecting my camera at all costs. Some other opportunist immediately stood on my carton. I told him to get off with such venom that he actually complied, and I tried again. The band were now onstage, and I began to shoot. But unless Ray came out on his ramp that extended into the crowd, I got nothing, and even then, I was shooting almost straight up. This would not do.

It was so loud and chaotic, and I had to think fast. I desperately looked around for an option. There was only one place to go. Between Ray and Dave Davies' ramps, there was a small triangular area in front of the stage, open but blocked from the crowd. Spanning it was a single raised two-by-four-foot beam. A-HA! If I could get there, the top of my head would be almost level to the stage.

I abandoned the crate and quickly made my way underneath the stage, the only way to get to the little pit. Two teenage security guards in yellow T-shirts stopped me despite my pass.

'Uh … you can't come here, miss.'

'I need to take photographs, and I can't see from the crowd. I just need to get to this right over …'

'Uh … you don't have the right pass.'

I could hear the band roaring above me, could feel the time swooshing by and I was getting a little nutty in the heat. I so badly didn't want to blow this opportunity.

'I'll be no trouble, just a few minutes and I'll leave! Please!'

'Uh, well, I dunno …'

Hesitation! YES! I went on with them for another minute or so and told them how grateful I was for their help. When I saw the boys look at each other questioningly, I yelled, 'THANKS, GUYS!' and bolted past them. I wriggled my way into the little pit, somehow hoisted myself onto the two-by-four board and balanced there for the rest of the show.

I was generously rewarded with some big smiles from Ray, very amused to see what I had done now. I gave him a smile and a thumbs-up as I began to shoot, jumping down into the darkness under the stage to change out film rolls in the camera and to wipe my sweaty hands and face on my shirt before scrambling up on the board again.

I knew I was getting great shots; I could feel it, and I was thrilled. Despite the band's seriously nasty mood amongst themselves that day, I caught Dave Davies looking over to his right at his brother with the biggest grin I have ever seen on him. Click! Years later, that became the cover shot of Dave's first *Unfinished Business* CD, which was issued in the UK. I took a glance behind me. More than 60,000 people, I thought, and I am here, getting splinters in my sore wobbling butt, dripping sweat and my favourite band right in front of me. I was one happy girl.

Edited from a 2008 post on Spellman's blog, *Popthomology* (popthomology.com).

Jim Smart – Honolulu, Hawaii, US

I first encountered The Kinks onstage in 1982. I had previously only known them from their records, which I played alone as a teenager in my bedroom. I discovered them in 1980, partly because of all the various Kinks covers that bands like The Pretenders, Van Halen and The Romantics were having success with. I bought their albums one at a time, tentatively at first. I remember how their sensitive side really got me with songs like 'Little Bit Of Emotion' and 'Sitting In My Hotel'. But my peers and I really wanted to hear loud distortion and bombastic power-pop, and The Kinks excelled at this. I bought *Give The People What They Want* on the day it was released, but I had never seen them live.

I went to the US Festival in California on my 18th birthday, excited to see all the best bands of the day, including two of my favourites, The Cars and The Kinks. The Cars stood perfectly still and played their songs so precisely that it was like playing their records with cardboard cutouts on stage. The Kinks were the opposite of that, another thing entirely. They stopped their songs in the middle, joked with each other, demanded audience participation, started songs over, did all their call-and-response tricks and changed the songs to keep things fresh and interesting. I learnt later how they battled with the concert organisers; I could feel various kinds of tension and aggression mixed in with their humour and musical power.

At this point, I was a very big Dave Davies fan, playing his *AFL1-3603* album on constant rotation. He was having a very good night at the US Festival, and it was wonderful to see him in person. Ray was in top form, in total command of that huge audience. He held us in the palm of his hand. The best moment was during 'The Hard Way' when I shouted my favourite part along with Ray Davies up on the stage: 'I'm wasting my vocation teaching you to write neat, when you're only fit to sweep the streets!' I remember how everyone around me turned to stare at me. What a weirdo. I didn't care. I'd found my favourite band.

John Riebow – Hatfield, Pennsylvania, US

My first and most vivid memory of seeing the Kinks live was the smoke that seemed to be steaming from Dave Davies' fingers as he played his blistering guitar solos during the band's energetic show in support of *Give The People What They Want* in the autumn of 1982. I had seen Pete Townshend play until his fingers bled, but Dave's motions were so fierce that his fingertips appeared to be on fire. Man, that had to hurt! And wouldn't it melt the guitar? I nudged my friend. He was just as awestruck as me. It was only when we studied Dave between songs that we realised it was not smoke but dust rolling in the air. The guitarist bathed his fingers in talcum powder at intervals so they would slide smoothly up and down the fretboard, resulting in pale clouds emanating from the instrument. What a cool trick! And it worked: notes bent and flowed like birds in flight.

The Kinks were at the height of their powers during the mid-1980s and 1990s live shows, and I was fortunate to have seen them a dozen times. The concerts often began with the chilling radio static intro that preceded 'Around The Dial' or the thrilling 'You Really Got Me' tease that bled into 'Do It Again' from *State Of Confusion*. The energy level was at 100% out of the gate, and that was just the beginning!

With such a strong catalogue behind them, every gig was like a greatest-hits show, each song a tasty morsel of rock 'n' roll genius. Ray was an engaging and entertaining frontman, playing flawless rhythm guitar while leaping around the stage, bathed in sweat, basking in the glow of his creations – self-deprecating, fey and charming, but the clear leader of the group. Jim Rodford and Mick Avory (later Bob Henrit) powered the beat, and Ian Gibbons filled the space around the Davies brothers' guitars with jingling keyboards and airy backing vocals. But my eyes were often on Dave, always dressed in black, with a pale face and long hair shimmering in the lights, laying down killer riffs that propelled the music into the stratosphere. He faded in and out of the light and dust clouds like a ghost, but his commanding guitar was ever-present.

I had been captivated by the band since my father introduced them to me when I was about five years old, so The Kinks have been part of the soundtrack of my life for half a century. It was a privilege to get to see the boys live while in my teens, and little did I realise I would later meet Ray at an in-store appearance at Tower Records. What drew me to The Kinks was not just the driving beat and engaging melodies but the heart of the songs: Ray's intelligent and thoughtful lyrics, which painted visions of what I thought English life to be, what I thought England was. From 'Victoria' to 'Well Respected Man' to 'Village Green Preservation Society' and 'Waterloo Sunset', The Kinks are an Anglophile's dream, recalling a time when Britain was great and there was a British Empire.

Kinks records always seem to be in heavy rotation around the house, but I always find myself returning to the live album that encapsulates my concert memories. One just has to listen to *One For The Road* (which has lived in my life as a cassette, vinyl record and well-worn CD) to appreciate the full power of their performances. You'll just have to imagine the smoke coming from Dave's fingers.

1984
Graham Morford – Plymouth, UK

I was working in London on a construction job in March 1984. The Kinks were playing that night at Guildford Civic Centre, an hour's train journey from London. I had tickets to see the band the next week for two consecutive nights at the Hammersmith Palais, but I was impatient and fancied trying to get to Guildford. During my tea break, I rang the box office at the Civic Centre to ask if they had any tickets for sale. They said the show was a sellout, but the local council were going to allow them a further 50 tickets that would go on sale that afternoon. I left the phone box, went back to the job and told my mate to tell the boss I had to see my accountant. Then, I headed to central London to get a train to Guildford. I got to the Civic Centre excited that I would be seeing The Kinks that evening. I went to the box office, but they didn't have the extra 50 tickets they had been promised – the council had changed their mind, and they didn't have any tickets for sale.

I was absolutely gutted. I walked around the Civic Centre, and there was a big tour bus parked around the back. I saw some people gathered around the stage door. I went up and joined them, and I could hear the band doing a soundcheck. They were playing 'The Hard Way', and even though I was outside the building, it sounded awesome. It was only a few minutes, but I consoled myself that at least I got to hear them play.

The music stopped, the doors opened and people started to come out. A few roadies emerged and then Dave Davies – people started to crowd around him for autographs. I saw some other people and recognised Ian Gibbons, Jim Rodford and a few heavies. I managed to get Dave Davies to sign something. Then Ray was there, and he had people milling around him. I shoved a scrap of paper at him, which he signed, and I quickly asked him if I could buy a ticket for the gig – they had said they would have more tickets on sale; that wasn't the case now, but I was happy to pay for one. Ray gestured to a guy who was giving people what appeared to be tickets and said, 'These people are fan club members from Germany and have arranged to meet us here to have complimentary tickets.' I hadn't noticed them at all.

I decided to give it one last shot. I felt uncomfortable, but I said to Ray, 'My grandad and your dad were best mates', hoping that somehow this would somehow change things. He carried on signing autographs, then looked up at me and said, 'Yeah? Who is your grandad, then?' I said, 'Fred Morford.' My dad was from Muswell Hill, and my grandad and Fred Davies (Ray and Dave's dad) were indeed best mates back in the day. There was a slight pause – then, amazingly, I saw a look of recognition on Ray's face, and he nodded. 'Yeah, I remember him. How's he doing?' I told him that, unfortunately, he had died a few years earlier. He said, 'I'm sorry to hear that.' Then, he called over to the man with the tickets: 'Give this guy one.' 'Oh wow – thanks, mate!' I said to Ray, who carried on signing autographs.

In a moment, I had gone from the depths of despair to complete and utter excitement and elation. I said my thanks again to the guy with the tickets as he put one into my hand. It was a satin embossed ticket with 'Kinks U.S. Tour 1980' stamped on it. Someone had written on it in marker pen: 'Out Front Only'. The gig was amazing!

The next week, I was with a mate outside the Hammersmith Palais before the Kinks gig. A car pulled up and a guy in an overcoat got out. It was Ray Davies being dropped off right outside the venue where his band were playing that night. He looked around. It was busy with people milling around, but nobody noticed him or reacted. He saw me, nodded and smiled, then walked through the crowd into the foyer of the Palais to do the gig. Me and Ray were now on nodding terms. In reality, I'm sure he didn't have a clue who I was – but he *did* nod.

Danny Osterweil – Pittsgrove, New Jersey, US

I saw the Kinks many times. I once took (by myself) a train from Philadelphia to Madison Square Garden in New York. It must have been the gig in December 1984. *Word Of Mouth* had just come out. I scalped a ticket when I got there and landed a seat viewing the left side of the stage. I got a view of the backstage area where Ray duked a security officer for throwing a fan into the audience. He then ran back onstage to continue his act of solid entertainment. I am not sure that any other fans witnessed what I did.

I was initially a Kinks fan back in the 1960s and rekindled my interest in the early 1980s. It was always so much fun to see them!

1985
Brent Hallenbeck – St. George, Vermont, US

My memory of my first and only Kinks concert on 18 September 1985 is a little fuzzy. I remember standing in the front row at the SUNY Plattsburgh fieldhouse and watching Ray Davies scamper off the stage for repeated costume changes. I recall almost nothing about the music other than that I enjoyed it. The setlist from that night that I found online does little to jog my memory – sure, there was 'You Really Got Me', 'Come Dancing', 'Lola' and 'Give The People What They Want', but five of the 16 songs are listed as 'unknown', which sums up my recollection as well.

The part of that night I do remember, however, is meeting Ray after the show.

He was my first songwriting hero. I loved the popular stuff but really dug what, at the time, were considered Kinks obscurities. The songs on *Village Green Preservation Society* and especially *Muswell Hillbillies* tell such vivid, melancholy stories. As a college English major who was all about telling vivid, melancholy stories, I saw Ray Davies as an icon, someone who could sum up life in a few lyrics with absolutely no words wasted.

I kept my boombox in my car in the fieldhouse parking lot. After the show, I went out to retrieve it and brought it backstage, where I asked a manager if I could get Ray to record an ID for the college radio station where I was a DJ. Ray came out shortly, listened to my request and then asked if I could write the station information down somewhere so he could read it. I reached for my wallet and pulled out a business card someone had given me recently. On the back, I wrote 'FM 94 WPLT'. Ray looked it over, I got the cassette tape rolling and he said, 'Hi, this is Ray Davies of The Kinks, and you're listening to FM 94 WPLT, Plattsburgh', drawing out the final syllable – 'buuuurrrggghhhh' – with that sonorous British accent of his. He handed the card back to me and went on his way. Nearly 40 years later, I still keep that business card in my wallet, with 'FM 94 WPLT' in black ink smudged slightly by the post-show sweat of my songwriting hero.

Hallenbeck has covered the Vermont entertainment scene for the *Burlington Free Press* since 2004.

Elaine A. Benjamin – Vestal, New York, US
I met my husband-to-be, Rich, in the summer of 1974 on my college campus in a class called Shakespeare's Tragedies. I was in my last semester before

graduating, and Rich was returning to college after serving a stint in the Army. One of the things that bound us together was The Kinks. When we met, we immediately began to talk about The Kinks. I soon discovered he had a great collection of Kinks albums – much better than my limited collection. Before long, he dragged my huge steamer trunk up to his second-floor apartment, and we've been together ever since.

We both graduated from college and moved to the Binghamton, New York, area in 1978. The Kinks performed at SUNY Binghamton on 20 September 1985, and we were thrilled to be able to see them in our own area. Since it was the start of the school year, a lot of freshmen attended. As we waited in the lobby for the concert to start, I noticed a tall blonde coed standing in front of me and recognised her as a next-door neighbour from home who I used to babysit. Boy, did I suddenly feel old!

There was an opening act that night and being jaded and older and realising we'd most likely be standing throughout the entire concert, we were content to stay comfortably seated in the lobby for a while. All of a sudden, we heard some very recognisable opening chords, looked at each other in shock and, without saying a word, high-tailed it into the venue! We elbowed our way through the crowd until we were in the front of the stage – and there were our beloved Kinks. Those kids must have been amused by these two seasoned working stiffs crashing through their ranks. I've never been that aggressive before or since! We would have been terribly disappointed if we couldn't have seen the band close up and would never have lived it down had we missed more than just a few bars of the opening song!

In 2023, my husband and I are still together after 49 years – thanks in great part to The Kinks, who helped to bring us together. We are both in our 70s and retired. Nowadays, we are thrilled when a Kinks question comes up on our nightly viewing of *Jeopardy* – of course, we always know the answer ... and phrase it in the form of a question! When we reflect on The Kinks, we relive our young and innocent days, and I am in paradise.

1986
Gerard van Calcar – Amsterdam, The Netherlands
When I was a teenager in the 1980s, I constantly played the music of my favourite band – The Kinks! My parents had no clue about them. Dad loved jazz, and Mum just liked songs she heard on the radio, mostly easy listening. She was fed up one day of constantly hearing our boys, and she told me there is more than just one band to explore. 'Okay,' I said, 'I am open to hearing suggestions. For example, what is your favourite song of all time?' She thought for a moment and then said: 'I love the song 'This Strange Effect', performed by Dave Berry, with his mysterious hands act.' Imagine the joy I had when telling her who wrote that lovely song!

1989
Laura Seel – Greensboro, North Carolina, US

'What are you gonna do, Laura?!' My friend's words ricocheted around my synapses.

In 1989, we traipsed around the Pittsburgh Airport Marriott in denim jackets and high-top Reeboks, chasing a tip from another concertgoer that The Kinks might be staying there that night. We spotted the Cahoots Lounge and riffed on the name, but as we passed the doorway, our swagger was snatched.

'I see Dave', my friend hissed.

'I see Ray', I hissed back. The band were seated at the back of the bar, laughing and chatting. Ray Davies glanced up as I flew past with a comically gaping jaw. We stalked them; we found them. Now what? Ignoring my cardiac warning signs, I strode into the bar.

'Good show, Ray', I said, as if I'm writing for *Creem*. Ray had kind eyes, and when they focused on you, everything else in the room melted into bokeh. I took in his black Zildjian shirt, blue ski jacket, white sweatpants, Corona bottle and the band-aid on his hand. My hero, flesh and blood.

I was out of words, so I asked for an autograph. His wife had to dig into her purse for a pen; I hadn't thought of that. I found it difficult to think. Ray asked my name and spelt it correctly. I asked if there was somewhere I could send him a letter. Sure, he said, I'll write the address on the back. (It was for Konk Studios in London.)

My friend snapped an amazing picture with her Kodak 110 camera. I thanked Ray and left the bar like I had better things to do. Wait. A once-in-a-lifetime chance to tell this man what he's meant to me and that's it?

I found a Marriott notepad and pen, and I wrote Ray a note, the contents of which are lost to time – by which I mean it's too silly to share.

Back to Cahoots. Ray watched me all the way over, as he did the first time.

'Hello', he said, with a warm smile.

'This says it better', I replied, offering the note.

'Thanks, love', he said, taking it from me. I smiled, pivoted on weak pegs and started to leave.

'Thanks, Laura', Ray called after me, like he meant it.

And you're starstruck, baby, starstruck.
You're taken in by the lights,
Think you'll never look back,
You know you're starstruck on me.
Don't you know that you are,
Starstruck on me.
And you always will be

'Hi Ray'. That's how each letter started, the ones written in cursive on both sides of the paper, folded neatly and hand-delivered through the mail slot at

Konk Studios in the fall of 1990.

I turned 21 that fall, 'studying' abroad in London. On a Friday, I'd take the Piccadilly line north to Turnpike Lane station, walk 20 minutes through Hornsey, park myself somewhere along Tottenham Lane and write Ray Davies a letter. They were mostly about nothing, the letters: colour commentary of my roommates' arguments over how loudly one should butter one's toast; accounts of our Hyde Park escapades the night before, fuelled by too much Strongbow cider at the pub; sightseeing plans for our fall break trip to Ireland; yearnings about the extraordinary life I wanted to live and words of adoration that, even in their adolescent excess, didn't fully express how much The Kinks' music, and Ray's songwriting, meant to me.

Sometimes, I'd wrap the letter around a bottle of Corona and gently drop that through the mail slot: a bribe to whoever was working in the studio, encouraging them to see that my letters got to Ray. The Coronas paid off.

We had a few Ray sightings, my friend and I, from our stakeout spots across from Konk – one of which, a nice passing gentleman pointed out, doubled as the dog relief area. One day, Ray walked right past us on the way to the corner shop. He said hello, then paused at the shop door.

'How was your trip to Ireland?' he said. Catching my breath, I told him we'd run out of money and didn't go. A few minutes later, Ray emerged from the shop with two packets of peanuts and handed them to us. 'It's all I'm having for lunch today, so here ...'

Whoever said never meet your heroes never met Raymond Douglas Davies.

> Everybody's looking for the sun.
> People strain their eyes to see
> But I see you and you see me,
> And ain't that wonder?

The 1990s

In 1990, their first year of eligibility, The Kinks were inducted into the Rock and Roll Hall of Fame, and all four original members – Ray Davies, Dave Davies, Mick Avory and Pete Quaife – accepted the honour. With his typical wry humour, Ray looked out at the audience in their tuxedoes and formal gowns, and he lamented how rock 'n' roll had become 'respectable'.

Dropped by MCA Records, the band landed their final major-label deal at Columbia in 1991, and the *Did Ya* EP featured a title track more 1960s-ish than they had sounded in years. *Phobia*, the full album that followed, alternated between hard rock and gentler slice-of-life pop tunes. Keyboardist Mark Haley departed the band before the *Phobia* sessions, and Ian Gibbons rejoined for the tour after its release.

Marketing for *Phobia* was haphazard, and with young grunge-rock bands ascendant, getting any attention proved difficult. The album peaked at number 166 on the *Billboard* charts, and Columbia cut The Kinks loose in 1994. Undeterred, they released a UK-only live album, *To The Bone*, on their own Konk label. It included concert tracks and stripped-down classics recorded at Konk Studios in front of a small audience from the Official Kinks Fan Club.

When an expanded two-CD version was released in the US through Guardian Records in 1996, it included the final two original Kinks songs to date: 'Animal' and 'To The Bone'.

Freed from recording contract obligations, The Kinks seemed more willing to look back at their 30-year career rather than record new material. Fans who attended concerts in the US, the UK and Japan in 1994 and 1995 almost unanimously describe a band in top form. Their final US concert in September 1995 was, appropriately enough, a benefit for the Rock and Roll Hall of Fame's opening weekend in Cleveland, Ohio.

Former Kinks members John Gosling, John Dalton and Mick Avory regrouped in 1994 with guitarist/lead singer Dave Clarke as the Kast Off Kinks. Other ex-Kinks – such as Ian Gibbons, Jim Rodford and Mark Haley – have performed with the group over the past 30 years, and they are booked annually for the Official Kinks Fan Club convention.

Ray Davies's 'unauthorised autobiography', *X-Ray*, was published in the UK in 1995, then a year later in the US; Dave Davies's book, *Kink*, came out in the UK in 1996, then a year later in the US. Both shared stories about the band's ups and downs, with Ray focused on his early life and The Kinks during the 1960s and early 1970s, while Dave covered up to the present.

The Kinks played their final shows in 1996 on 1 June at the 12 Timmar 70-tal ('12 Hours of '70s Music') festival in Sweden and on 15 June at the Norwegian Wood Festival in Norway. There was no formal announcement of a band split, and discussions about getting back together onstage or in the studio (sometimes even about reuniting with Mick and Pete) continued for a few years but never came to fruition.

Ray's in-store book readings, which included a few songs, evolved into *20th Century Man*, a stage show with guitarist Pete Mathison. US television network VH-1 filmed a performance at the Westbeth Theatre in New York City in early 1996 to launch its new programme, *Storytellers*, which ran with a similar format of songs and personal anecdotes for 98 episodes over the next 19 years. Ray's stage show was renamed *The Storyteller*, with a live album released under that name in 1998.

Dave formed a solo band with musicians from Los Angeles (where he was based at the time) and began to tour around the US. Velvel Records released a career-spanning compilation, *Unfinished Business*, in 1999, with a new title track paying tribute to John Lennon.

In 1998, Ray published *Waterloo Sunset*, a collection of short stories based on selected songs and a few unreleased tracks; an accompanying two-CD set of The Kinks' greatest hits and songs from the book was also released. A modified version of the book came out in the US in 2000, with some stories added, dropped or revised.

As Britpop took over the UK charts in the mid-1990s, bands such as Blur and Oasis hailed The Kinks as 'godfathers'.

Albums by The Kinks: *Did Ya* EP (1991), *Phobia* (1993), *To The Bone* (1994/1996)
Album by Ray Davies: *The Storyteller* (1998)
Albums by Dave Davies: *Village Of The Damned* soundtrack with John Carpenter (1995), *Unfinished Business* (1999), *Fortis Green* (1999)

1990
Around The Dial With ... Neil Ottenstein

My Kinks story must have started in the early 1970s (possibly 1973). On one of our trips to England to visit my grandparents in Stanmore on the outer skirts of London, I bought (or received) the album *The Most Of Herman's Hermits* on the Pye label. My brother and I enjoyed the song 'I'm Henry VIII, I Am'. When playing the album on my record player, I noticed that one song, 'Dandy', was written by someone named Davies. For some reason, this stuck out, and I thought he was the best of the writers they had. Parallel to this, I remember listening to The Doors' song 'Hello, I Love You'. This quickly became my favourite of theirs.

In late 1976, my brother and I, on one of our many trips to the Greenwich library to borrow records, came across *Everybody's In Show-Biz*. My brother told me that I would like the album and the group The Kinks. He was most definitely correct. Several weeks later, I was listening to *Things From England*, Scott Muni's wonderful programme on Friday afternoons on WNEW-FM (one of the best music radio programs in my memory), when he played songs from the upcoming Kinks album, *Sleepwalker*.

Sometime later, I discovered the Davies of 'Dandy' was Ray Davies and that the song had been given to Herman's Hermits before The Kinks could release it as their own single. At some other time, I discovered (probably from reading Lillian Roxon's *Rock Encyclopedia*) that 'Hello, I Love You' was based on the Kinks hit 'All Day And All Of The Night'.

Over the years, we borrowed more Kinks albums from the library, and my brother bought me other Kinks albums for my birthday. I remember looking at an old *Stereo Review* magazine and seeing *Muswell Hillbillies* had been awarded album of the year in 1971. I searched for more albums at the various record stores.

In 1990, after noticing various music polls in the Usenet group rec.music.misc about other bands, I decided to run one for The Kinks. While sending out the results on 6 February, I added:

> By the way, I was thinking of trying to start a Kinks mailing list. If you are interested in being on this list, send me an e-mail message saying so. I am probably not the best person to be starting this, as I hope to be finishing up here this semester, but I can at least start things up and someone else can take over later if there is interest.

There was a good response, and the list was started. Even after graduating, my email account was kept alive, and I was able to keep the list running. At the end of 1994, the members of the list decided to turn it into a digest mailing list. I'm still running the list. One of the main goals was to learn more about The Kinks and to spread news about them. That has been accomplished, and I am grateful to all the members of the list over all the years.

Ottenstein lives in Bowie, Maryland, US. To learn more about the Kinks Preservation Society mailing list and to view the archives, go online and find kindakinks.net/maillist.

Roel Dijksterhuis – Ten Boer, The Netherlands

During all my years as a Kinks fan, so many songs (too many to mention) have helped me during sad times and happy times in my life.

> Moments of ecstatic happiness
> And the moments of stress that we had better forget

There was always Kinks music to relax me and give me new energy. In January 1990, when my dad – my dear friend and helper – suddenly died at almost 67 years old, it felt like my life was ending. As a good Christian and believer in God, I asked him for help, and he gave me the strength to go on.

During that time, I played Kinks records to clear my mind, and I had just bought the CDs *UK Jive* and *Sleepwalker*. While listening to 'Life Goes On', I heard:

Life will hit you, when you're unprepared,
Life will hit you when you least expect it
but life goes on and on and on

Furthermore, in 'Now And Then', I heard:

One day we'll be born again
Our lovers and friends will remain
To live in a world without suffering and pain

And, of course, those beautiful lyrics in my all-time favourite song, 'Days', meant a lot to me:

Thank you for the days
Those endless days, those sacred days you gave me
I'm thinking of the days
I won't forget a single day, believe me
And though you're gone
You're with me every single day, believe me
Days I'll remember all my life ...

After hearing those songs, again and again, I became more and more accepting. I could face the fact that my father was gone and that I had lost a dear friend, but that my 'life goes on'.

Adapted from a letter Dijksterhuis wrote to Ray and Dave Davies in the 1990s.

Igor Znidarsic – Utrecht, The Netherlands

The news came from my good friend Martijn: The Kinks were coming to Leuven in Belgium. For us Dutch people, that's just around the corner. He had already bought two tickets.

I had been a fan since 1976. I was still in high school when, one day, I put a borrowed *Muswell Hillbillies* record on my turntable. Wow! That music! And those lyrics! I also lived a 'Complicated Life', had the 'Acute Schizophrenia Paranoia Blues' and was a '20th Century Man'. I had tears in my eyes during 'Oklahoma USA' – so unbelievably beautiful. I played the record 12 times in a row – insatiable.

My classmate Martijn, who already was a Kinks fan, heard about it and invited me to his house, where he played me more of the band's work. It was the start of a lifelong addiction.

The first time I saw them live was at Pinkpop in 1977. In the years that followed, Martijn and I worked for the Dutch fan club, we attended nearly all concerts in the Netherlands and Belgium, and we met band members several times backstage and in hotels. In Brussels in 1980, Ray introduced us to his girlfriend, who I later realised was Chrissie Hynde. Few knew about the relationship at the time. The last time they played in the Netherlands was in Beurs van Berlage in Amsterdam in 1993.

A few years earlier (15 August 1990), I saw them in Leuven, not knowing it would be almost my last Kinks concert ever. The concert was at Oude Markt, which turns out to be a small square surrounded by classical buildings. It was accessible on one side only, with crowd barriers placed a short distance from the stage. As the square filled up, the pressure in the front, where we stood, increased. I felt pushing in my back, and I got squeezed. The band entered the stage, above which dark clouds had gathered. After a few songs, the ever-increasing pressure from all sides made it more and more difficult for me to breathe. Martijn had the same problem – I could see the panic in his eyes.

A girl, two heads shorter than me, looked up at me desperately, and then I saw her eyes roll back as she fainted. With a few men, we lifted her above our heads and pushed her forward. Elsewhere, someone else was being carried away. People started shouting at the guards who were standing between the stage and the crush barriers: 'Give us some room! Take those crush barriers away! We're suffocating here!' Someone else shouted: 'Don't let any more people enter the square!' The guards seemed to hear it, but they hesitated to act.

Out of nowhere, the dark clouds unloaded, the cold rain coming down in buckets. I was soaked to the skin in no time. The crowd pressure became frightening. I felt like a sardine in a can and could hardly breathe. 'This is not going to end well', I thought, desperately trying to keep calm to save my last bits of oxygen.

Suddenly, I had an idea. I was a journalist, and my press card might still be in my inside pocket. I felt inside, and indeed it was. I stretched myself as tall as I could and shouted, waving the press card above my head, 'I'm a journalist! I have to go to the stage!' I kept shouting until I got the attention of a guard. 'I work for a music magazine!' It was a lie because I actually worked for a food magazine. The guard peered at the press card, which said 'PRESS' in big letters. He hesitated for a moment, then walked forward and beckoned me.

Roughly pushing people aside and stepping on their feet, I squeezed myself toward the crush barriers, followed by Martijn. The guard made a small opening, and we slipped through. While Dave blasted the 'You Really Got Me' riff across the square, I took a few deep breaths, then I said to Martijn: 'Dying at a Kinks concert … it could be worse.' He laughed faintly and replied: 'Which song would you choose?' I'm still thinking about that.

1992
Rory Collins – Brockley, London, UK

I've been a massive Kinks fan since I heard 'Sunny Afternoon' coming out of my dad's speakers on his battered old Bush record player when I was a young kid.

Left: Gerrit van den Berg gave Dave Davies a miniature that he created of 6 Denmark Place, Ray and Dave Davies' childhood home. (*Provided by Gerrit van den Berg*)

Right: Vincent de Waal watched through the window of the Proud Galleries in London as Ray Davies was interviewed by Nina Nannar for ITV News in October 2018. (*Vincent de Waal*)

Left: Martin Hutchinson (centre) enjoys a pint with Mick Avory (left) and John Dalton (right). Hutchinson wrote *On Track … The Kinks* for Sonicbond Publishing. (*Provided by Martin Hutchinson*)

Right: Dave Davies performs at the Bull Run in Shirley, Massachusetts, US, on 30 May 2013. (*Diane Germano*)

Below: James Swartz sings onstage with Dave Davies during a concert at City Winery in New York City on 12 November 2013. (*Dawn Badessa*)

Above: After the 2009 Dutch fan meeting in Utrecht. From left to right: Rob Kopp, Huub Goudzwaard, Mick Avory, Debi Doss, Ian Gibbons, Simon van den Bergh, Dave Clarke, Jim Rodford, Ray Davies, Karin Forsman, Ruud Kerstiens and Dick van Veelen. (*Provided by Dick van Veelen*)

Left: Kasia Kaszkowiak got to know Ray Davies – and London – thanks to her love of The Kinks. (*Provided by Kasia Kaszkowiak*)

Right: As part of their Kinks documentary *Two For The Road*, Rob Peirson (left) and Lloyd Jansen visited the location where the promotional film for 'Dead End Street' was filmed in 1966. (*Provided by Rob Peirson*)

Below: Ray Davies and Dave Clarke perform during the 2009 Dutch fan meeting at Rockcafe Stairway to Heaven in Utrecht. (*Simon van den Bergh*)

Left: Ray Davies performs at the Capitol Center for the Arts in Concord, New Hampshire, US, on 23 September 2001. (*Diane Germano*)

Below: Many Kinks fans attended Ray Davies' songwriting courses in the 1990s and 2000s, including this one in November 2001 in Totleigh Barton, Cornwall, UK. (*Provided by Julia Reinhart*)

Right: Carey Fleiner wove a guitar strap for Dave Davies and presented it to him as a gift. (*Carey Fleiner*)

Below: At the age of eight, Evan Spellman had his first live Kinks experience at a Dave Davies concert in 2000 at the Sit 'n' Bull Pub in Massachusetts, US. (*Marianne Spellman*)

Above: In 1998, René Smits talked his way into Konk Studios in London – until someone called the studio manager. (*Provided by René Smits*)

Left: David Temple, co-founder and musical director for the Crouch End Festival Chorus, first met Ray Davies in 1998. They have had a fruitful musical partnership ever since. (*Provided by David Temple*)

Right: Ray Davies performs at the Oakdale Theater in Wallingford, Connecticut, US, on 22 October 1997. (*Diane Germano*)

Left: Dave Davies performs at Toad's Place in New Haven, Connecticut, US, on 2 December 1997. (*Joanne Corsano*)

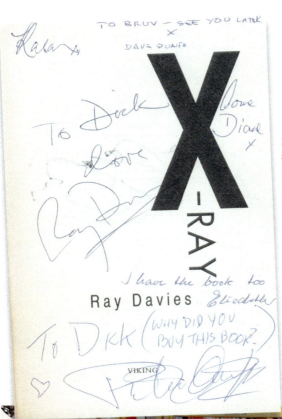

Left: Dick van Veelan has asked dozens of people associated with The Kinks to sign his copy of Ray Davies' autobiography *X-Ray*, including Pete Quaife and Rasa Davies. (*Dick Van Veelan*)

Below: Ray Davies signs Paul Como's copy of *X-Ray* at the Shakespeare & Company bookstore in New York City in October 1995. (*Provided by Paul Como*)

Right: In 1991, Konrad Kauczor attended a concert afterparty at a hotel in Hamburg, Germany, where Ray Davies entertained fans by playing Kinks songs and other tunes on the piano. (*Konrad Kauczor*)

Below: Portrait painter Igor Babailov (on the right) knew original Kinks bassist Pete Quaife not as a musician but as a fellow artist. (*Provided by Igor Babailov*)

Left: Photographer Marianne Spellman found herself in an awkward spot while Ray Davies performed with The Kinks on 19 June 1982 at JFK Stadium in Philadelphia. (*Marianne Spellman*)

Right: Laura Seel writes a letter to Ray Davies in 1990 while sitting on the steps of Konk Studios in London. (*Provided by Laura Seel*)

Above: Bernard De Gioanni (founder of the Kinks French Konnektion) greets Ray Davies at the airport in Nice, France, in 1980. (*Provided by Bernard De Gioanni*)

Left: Dave Davies on the train from Nice to Lyon in December 1980. (*Bernard De Gioanni*)

Right and below: The Kinks French Konnektion ran from 1977-84 and produced the fanzine *Kuppa Kinks*. (*Provided by Bernard De Gioanni*)

Right: The Kinks perform at a May 1968 Kinks concert in Vlagtwedde, The Netherlands. (*Ruud Kerstiens*)

Left: Rich Tanenbaum painted a *Schoolboys In Disgrace*-inspired mural outside his dorm room in the mid-1970s at Union College in Schenectady, New York, US. (*Provided by Rich Tanenbaum*)

Left: Ray Davies backstage before a 1968 Kinks concert in Vlagtwedde, The Netherlands. (*Ruud Kerstiens*)

Right: Dave Davies backstage before a 1968 Kinks concert in Vlagtwedde, The Netherlands. (*Ruud Kerstiens*)

Left: Pete Quaife backstage before a 1968 Kinks concert in Vlagtwedde, The Netherlands. (*Ruud Kerstiens*)

Right: Dave Davies in front of The Kinks' tour bus in Sacramento, California, US, in 1965. Sam Curtis, the band's road manager, is on the left. (*V. Mary Carroll*)

Left: Mick Avory beside The Kinks' tour bus in Sacramento, California, US, in 1965. (*V. Mary Carroll*)

Right: Olga Ruocco's correspondence with Pete Quaife often included drawings. After leaving The Kinks, he had a career as a graphic artist. (*Olga Ruocco*)

Fast-forward to 1992, age 20, I answered an ad in the UK's *Sunday Observer* to attend 'a five-day songwriting course tutored by ... Ray Davies.' I wrote and was accepted, and I soon found myself tearing up the motorway with my guitar on the back seat.

It was an excellent course, and Ray not only taught and offered advice, but he joined us for dinners and evening jams and chats in a Norfolk farmhouse. Also in attendance was Kimberly Rew, the guitarist in Katrina and the Waves, who had already penned 'Walking On Sunshine' – a talented and humble guy. Ray was great and perfect as a musical mentor, and he soon became that 'cool tutor' type (as opposed to a pretentious rock-star type), so any nerves quickly evaporated. He was personable and funny and enjoyed mixing with the 12 or so students who attended.

Late one evening, I tried to impress him with my knowledge of more obscure Kinks tunes like 'Moments', 'Lavender Hill' and 'Rosemary Rose'. According to one of the organisers, he was really touched that a '20-year-old kid' knew all his stuff.

A few years later, I was lucky enough to attend Konk Studios for some 'unplugged' recordings for what became 1994's *To The Bone*. As I sat in the small audience, Ray looked over at me and said, 'Hey, Rory! How's it going?' I was flattered that he had remembered me. Meanwhile, Dave asked me to hold up the lyrics to 'Death Of A Clown' for him to sing. Quite a good afternoon, by all accounts!

I'm 52 now and haven't forgotten a second of that experience.

Around The Dial With ... Wesley Stace
A Fan Speaks

I met Ray Davies in a Danish airport
Turned out to be a real nice guy
He said 'Keep writing your songs, man
As long as you can'
And I think that was good advice
But actually he didn't quite say that
I added that word 'man'
I'm just following his good words
But of course I'm a very big fan
And I was just trying to make this thing scan

I met many a famous person
I'm not gonna drop any names
Sure, I did mention Ray
When I started to play
But that's cos he is a credit to fame
Unlike a few I could mention

Who actually quite freaked me out
They treated me like I was one of those guys
Who carries a small gun about

So congratulations to those of you
Who feel the need to congratulate your heroes
It may be tense for both of you
But I'm sure they appreciate the gesture
But commiserations to souls that are lost
Who feel that murder is a way to get their love across
Great God above keep the people we love
From those merely seeking attention

Yes, I know what it's like to be bothered
And I know what it's like to be tired
But you gotta hide
In some kinda disguise
To be famous and yet be walked by
So, stars, watch your manners around me
You don't have to talk to me long
I may not pull a gun out on you
But I might write you into this song

Stace is a British novelist and singer-songwriter who has recorded more than two dozen albums as John Wesley Harding and under his own name. 'A Fan Speaks' was originally released on the 1998 album 'Dynablob 2: It Happened Every Night'. Lyrics reprinted with the kind permission of TOWNSONGS.

1993
Alan Binder – Whitestone, New York, US

This story took place at the Westbury Music Fair, a theatre-in-the-round in Westbury, NY, around 1993. When the show was about to start, a staff member took the band down one of the many aisles that went to the stage. During the show, the stage moved about 180 degrees in a semicircle. At the end of the set, our heroes seemed confused about which aisle would return them to 'backstage' and no staff member came to their rescue. So, instead, they hung out and shuffled around by their equipment on the side of the stage as we called for an encore. They obliged, and when the show was complete, a staff member finally led them back to their green room. I call it 'The Kinks having their *Spinal Tap* moment'.

Around The Dial With ... Igor Babailov

One day in 1993, while I was in my studio in Canada, the phone rang. I answered it, and a man introduced himself as 'Peter'. He was calling from an art gallery just down the street from my studio. He said that he stood in front of my painting, which was a portrait of an old man with a white beard that I exhibited there. He really liked the painting and wanted to meet me, and he asked if I could come to the gallery.

The gallery was a narrow, corridor-like space, and my painting hung at the very far end of it on the back wall. Upon entering the gallery, I went straight to my painting, and when I approached it, I saw a man standing next to it. At first, he looked at me with indifference, but when he realised that I could be the artist he was waiting for, he became visibly surprised and even expressed sincere doubt for a moment. He thought the old man in the painting was a self-portrait of the artist and was fully expecting to meet this old man with a white beard. Instead, there was a young lad in front of him – me. I was 28 years old and did look very young. Anyhow, he liked this painting, and now he was totally impressed because I was so young.

He introduced himself as Pete Quaife and, from that moment, we remained friends for almost 20 years until Pete's untimely death in 2010. When I met Pete, his name didn't tell me anything about his background because, growing up in the Soviet Union and behind the Iron Curtain, we knew about The Beatles and a few other bands, but The Kinks were somehow filtered out.

Although Pete was a 'celebrity' and truly earned this title, he was always down to earth and never looked down on others. He had the finest sense of humour that everyone around him absolutely loved. He had a passion for music (particularly classical music) and outstanding skill in playing guitar; he was a talented visual artist and astronomer who knew the name of every crater on the Moon; and, not to forget, he had a sophisticated taste for gourmet cooking.

He often had friends over at his home, and he visited my studio, too. In 1994, I asked him if he would sit for me for his portrait, and he enthusiastically agreed. He ended up standing for it, though, and it turned out to be a very fast portrait sketch (about two hours), done in one breath, and – most importantly – entirely from life.

Babailov is a portrait artist who is called a 'living master' by his contemporaries. He has painted three living presidents of three countries, two living prime ministers, members of noble families and British royalty and three living popes for the Vatican. He lives in Nashville, Tennessee, US. Learn more at babailov.com.

1994
Around The Dial With ... Dave Emlen
Back in the early 1980s, a friend from school had a Timex Sinclair 1000 computer (similar to a Sinclair ZX81 in the UK). It cost $99 at the time, and you connected it to your TV to write programs in BASIC. As we played with it, I got the idea to input album and song titles by The Kinks. My program would show you a menu of album titles, and when you picked one, it would

show you a list of song titles. I wanted to add lyrics, but with only 2K of RAM and the difficulty of typing on the tiny membrane keyboard, I wasn't going to get very far. My friend suggested putting a pause statement of two or three seconds in the program just before it would output the list of song titles. That way, it would look like the computer was hard at work, searching a massive database. We did that and were thrilled and amused by the results. It's funny that I've spent my career as a computer systems administrator trying to keep them running quickly and efficiently, yet one of my first computer experiences was purposely slowing it down!

About a dozen years later, at the university where I work, some faculty wanted to play around with this 'World Wide Web' thing that was catching on at some academic institutions. They asked me to set up a 'html server' for them. I started playing with it as well and soon realised that I now had the ability to implement my vision of a Kinks album/song 'database' with not only song lyrics but album cover images as well. I got busy scanning in CD cover artwork (LPs were too big for the scanner) and spent many hours typing in lyrics. Some albums came with song lyric sheets, which helped tremendously. For other albums... well, I did my best, and despite help later from fellow fans, I'm sure there are typos and misheard lyrics on the site to this day (as well as in the CD booklets of various album reissues since record companies would copy and paste from my site without first warning me).

I launched my website in March 1994 by sharing the URL on Neil Ottenstein's Kinks email digest. I had to explain what a website was and how to use a browser to view it. It wasn't long before I started hearing from fellow Kinks fans from all over the world who were visiting the website, and that was (and still is) the coolest thing about running it. Those fans started asking questions about the band – wanting to know tour dates or if there were any new recordings on the horizon. In those days, information about The Kinks was hard to come by, as it seemed traditional media (radio, TV and magazines) largely ignored them. I decided to add a page to my website to collect any current information I could find or that other fans sent to me. Since I had no way to verify anything, I called the page 'News & Rumors'. It turned into the most visited page on the site.

In these days of social media, where news and information about The Kinks are readily available elsewhere, I'm sure my website doesn't see anywhere close to the traffic it had in the late 1990s and 2000s. But I still hear from Kinks fans who visit the site, and I still get a kick out of it, so I'll keep it running for the foreseeable future.

Emlen lives in Rochester, New York, US. See his website at kindakinks.net.

Tracy Noonan – Amsterdam, The Netherlands

In March 1994, on the tenth anniversary of winning a Pretenders trip to Dallas, Texas, I got a call from Ginger Studios. They wanted me to be Ray

Davies' 'superfan' for their show *Don't Forget Your Toothbrush*. Wondering who would play a trick like this and how they got my number, I played along. The lady described the show, and eventually, it was clear this was not a joke. A few months earlier, at a Kinks show in Germany, I showed Ray some of my pictures. He chuckled at what I wrote on the Berlin Wall ('RAY Davies and tRAcY Noonan = Lust'). I brought that photo to the show because I think that laugh prompted him to make me his superfan.

I told her I would be in London in two weeks for The Kinks' gig at Wembley Arena. She said the show was that Saturday, and they would fly me in from Amsterdam. I would need to bring a personal item to give to Ray if he won the quiz. She listed items that superfans had brought in the past. I was looking around the room, and just as she said, 'stuffed animal', I was looking at the kitty that my sister, Beth, had given me.

Three days later, I got off the plane in London to find a nice man holding a yellow sign with my name on it. Good thing it wasn't spelt the way it was on my dressing room door ('NOONUN'), or I might have missed him. The driver first took me to my room at the Grosvenor House Hotel and then to London Studios. After the rehearsals (one with a stand-in and one with Ray), Ray's wardrobe lady, Julie, gave me a *Phobia* t-shirt. She told me Ray wanted me to have it and maybe I could wear it on the show. I decided to stay with the dress I'd brought.

I was overwhelmed when my 'assistant' led me onto the stage. Then Ray, bandleader Jools Holland and the band played 'You Really Got Me', and I started jammin'. Some of the audience could see me dancing and started laughing and clapping. The stage rotated to face the audience, and Ray joined me with host Chris Evans for the superfan quiz. I was nervous yet comforted by being onstage with my hero. It was the best night of my life, but I was glad when those five minutes were over!

In the green room, I watched the rest of the live broadcast with the contestants from the earlier segments and crew members. Eventually, Ray and his then-wife, Pat, came by. We talked a bit, and I repeatedly thanked Ray for such an amazing experience. He specifically wanted a picture with the two of us, so we posed for one – but I later discovered the film had run out! I'm still grumbling about that.

Two weeks later, at the Kinks' Wembley Arena concert, one guy recognised me and asked for my autograph! His friends thought, 'Why not? It might be worth money someday.' Backstage after the concert, drummer Bob Henrit told me that Konk Studios asked him if he knew how to contact me so I could do the show. He told them all he knew was that I worked for a diamond factory in Amsterdam. Someone there remembered a 'Happy DAVE Day' fax I'd sent the month before from work on the company stationery, which had a big diamond on it. Ginger Television called my employer, who, since I was off from work that day, gave them my home number. What an incredible chain of events that led to the most amazing night of my life!

You can see the *Don't Forget Your Toothbrush* superfan quiz at *youtube.com/watch?v=hkPz99ztdUg*.

Around The Dial With … Bill Orton

I had a phone call from Official Kinks Fan Club secretary Earl Law on Saturday 9 April 1994, asking if I would be available on Monday afternoon. He didn't want to tell me the reason, but after some pushing, he revealed it was an invite to Konk Studios with The Kinks. I managed to include my wife, Julie, and young son, Jon, and we were given the instructions to meet at Dick's Bar, a short walk away from Konk at 3 pm.

We duly arrived in good time, and our party totalled 14 chosen fans, including about four who were on the fan club team at that time. After some time, we were told that the band were aware we had arrived and would send for us shortly. One hour turned into two, and so it went on with various Konk staff coming over at intervals to update us and let us know we had not been forgotten. We also learned that both Ray and Dave were actually barred from the bar premises!

The evening pressed on, and some were considering going home when, around 10 pm, we were finally taken over and greeted by Ray, who informed us they just needed some adjustments, and we would be in the studio. Around 10:30 pm, we were led through some curtains over a doorway into what is called the Konk 'Live Room', which was the larger of the studios (the raised control room you see in the 'State Of Confusion' video was still there but disused at this time). Ray and Dave were in front of a set background to appear as if playing in the old front room at their childhood home. Ian Gibbons was to one side with an upright piano, organ and accordion; Jim Rodford was near the new control room, with Bob Henrit in a drum isolation booth (apparently, he had been there from midday).

We were spread around the studio room, and they began with a new version of 'Do You Remember Walter?' – at that point, I think we all realised this was very special! Another take of 'Walter' and then three takes of 'Death Of A Clown'. When I say it was that song and Dave on *Top Of The Pops* that really cemented it for me back in 1967, you will understand how much this moment meant to me. They did a nice version of 'Too Much On My Mind' with Ray and Dave on vocals and four takes of 'Uncle Son', none of which made the album. 'See My Friends' was interesting because they played over a pre-recorded backing track, so the take you hear on the album is how it was live in the studio. Other tracks included 'Apeman', 'Tired Of Waiting', 'Muswell Hillbilly', 'Gallon Of Gas' and 'Set Me Free' – by which time we were heading toward 2 am! The camera crew wanted to leave, and Ray announced, 'It's a wrap', leading the band through 'Sea Of Heartbreak', 'Singing The Blues' and 'C'mon Arsenal' (to the music of 'Twist And Shout'). Ray, Dave and the band were happy to sign items for us, and we all made our way home.

One funny moment: at one point, Ray asked his young guitar tech for his Martin D28 and told us that this was his prized guitar possession, having used it on 'Lola', 'Celluloid Heroes' and a host of others. At the same time, there was a breakdown in the control room, which almost sent Ray into a flip. He stood, let the guitar crash to the floor and marched into the control room to find out what they were doing! Fortunately, the guitar and session continued.

To say this was the ultimate fan gig would be an understatement, and despite the hours kept waiting and the long drive home, it was worth every moment. We had to wait another 18 years for any of the film to be screened in the *Echoes Of A World* documentary, and I understand that most of it has been edited and restored – but getting it released in any sort of full format is a big 'if'.

Orton has been the secretary of the Official Kinks Fan Club since 1996. He lives in Grendon, Warwickshire, UK.

Miriam Moore – Clinton, New York, US

Walking around the student activities fair in 1994 during my freshman year in college, the campus radio station caught my eye: KRRC, Radio Reed College – one of the first homes of Dr. Demento. Hmm, what to do, what to do?

Not that there was much suspense. My mom loved regaling friends with stories of my first rock concert: The Kinks, circa 1980, shaking my diapered butt to the music while hanging on to the balcony railing. I wish I remembered. 'Ducks On The Wall' was part of my childhood soundtrack. I think childhood officially ended when I understood that Ray was saying, 'I love you, baby, but I can't ball' instead of 'I can't fall'. Suddenly, I knew what he meant and was horrified. I played my parents' LPs over and over. My dad had all of them, and my mom only had the late 1970s albums, so 'Hay Fever', 'Life Goes On' and 'National Health' are anthems for me. My dad didn't like *Preservation*, so it wasn't until college, as I slowly built my CD collection at Portland's fabulous music stores, that I got to follow Mr. Flash's journey – and I loved it.

'What's your show going to be called?' asked the wise upperclassman taking my info down on the radio station signup. 'Um…' I hesitated – I didn't know. I never had DJ ambitions, and they told me I'd have a bad timeslot to start, so how do I get people to listen? Ah ha! Inspiration struck: What college student doesn't love a good play on words? And if sex is involved, all the better. 'Kinky Thoughts', I said confidently.

During my junior year abroad in England, I saw Ray Davies' solo show in London, met superfan Olga Ruocco and became friends, and introduced her to the Kinks email digest. I met Ray a few times, barely able to speak, and got him to sign an original copy of the 'You Really Got Me' sheet music (hastily procured at a shop in Norwich) for my dad. Then Mick Avory showed up to watch Ray's show, so I got him to sign the sheet music, too – OH MY GOSH, talk about winning. I could never have talked to them or asked for their autographs for myself, but for my dad, I could muster up the courage.

Then on to grad school in Boston, and the fortuitous connection of noticing Jill Brand's email address and realising she was at the school where I was about to start. Jill welcomed me into her family with many wonderful music and sports memories. One of the greatest weekends of my life was when Dad visited me in Boston, and we – plus Jill Brand and her family, along with Kate Hunter – saw Dave Davies several times at the Sit 'n' Bull Pub in Maynard. Seeing Dave that close to my dad (also a Dave) was a heart-filling time and will always be a special memory.

Years later, my wife forwarded me an invitation for summer DJ stints at Hamilton College, her institution. 'Kinky Thoughts' was reborn, though with internet streaming and the regulations that go with it. What do you mean, only three songs by the same artist in a two-hour show!?! That stretched my creativity, but I found joy in weaving different artists around and between The Kinks, plus Ray and Dave solo. It was justification for buying all the 'kovers' I could find.

The Kinks Preservation Society email list has brought so many wonderful people into my life, both digitally and virtually – Carl Biancuchi, Bud Stafford, Neil Ottenstein, Frank Lima and more. 'Days I'll remember all my life'. That's what The Kinks are for me – a soundtrack, sure, but more a point of connection to many special people, starting with my parents and especially my dad, and then flowing into the river of fans far and wide. I can't imagine my life without them.

Around The Dial With ... Dick Van Veelen

In October 1994, Ray Davies hosted a signing for his book *X-Ray* at the Muswell Hill Bookshop (since closed). I found out and sent a letter to the bookshop asking Ray to sign a copy for me. My request was granted, and I received the book with Ray's signature and the dedication: 'To Dick, with love.' This book was the first signed item in my Kinks collection. I took it with me wherever anything to do with The Kinks was organised to have it signed by members of the band, members of the Davies family and various people associated with the band. I am convinced that there are few items with so many signatures of people linked to The Kinks.

I collected most of the signatures during the English and Dutch fan meetings. In Holland, I was a member of the board of The Dutch Kinks Preservation Society, which organised fan meetings from 1999 to 2014 at Rockcafé Stairway to Heaven in Utrecht and at Poppodium Estrado in Harderwijk, where I met several band members. The meetings were attended by fans from home and abroad, including England, Germany, France, Norway and the US.

Pete Quaife, with his sense of humour, signed with this comment in 2004: 'Why did you buy this book?' In November 2010, five months after his brother's death, Dave Quaife added his signature and wrote: 'To bruv – see you later.' This came true when he died in April 2023.

Backup singers from the 1970s also signed. Shirlie Roden wrote: 'May the Mirror of Love shine on you.' Debi Doss had a less poetic quote: 'From one of the silly old tarts', as band members called the ladies at the time.

Geoff Edgers, star of the documentary film *Do It Again*, wrote at the International Film Festival in Rotterdam in 2010: 'Never stop loving The Kinks and wishing, like we all do, that they will one day play together again.'

Another special one: Dave Berry, who had a huge hit in Holland with Ray's composition, 'This Strange Effect'. It spent 35 weeks in the Dutch charts, taking it into pop history as one of the longest-listed hits. He predictably signed with 'Strange Effect'.

And finally, the Davies brothers. I asked Dave to sign his autograph after his memorable performance at Islington Assembly Hall in December 2015. He did so with a black felt pen on the other side of the page on which Ray had signed. The ink pressed through Ray's signature. Again, the brothers kept bothering each other! But fortunately, Ray signed my book again in 2008 after the musical *Come Dancing* at Theatre Royal Stratford East. There I also met Gwen, Peggy and Dorothy – sisters of Ray and Dave – and they also immortalised their names in my book.

The Dutch Kinks Preservation Society organised the first fan meeting in 1999 with The Kast Off Kinks, and they performed with various lineups until 2014. We brought almost all The Kinks' band members to Holland, except unfortunately for Dave. Even Ray stayed with us for a weekend in 2009. The theme was the 40th anniversary of the *Arthur* album. And what fan can say he dined with his idol?

Pete Quaife also came to the occasional fan convention, such as a 2004 event in Utrecht, where he played with The Kast Off Kinks and read extracts from his unpublished rock 'n' roll novel *Veritas* (eventually published in 2010). After Pete's death in 2010, *The Guardian* posted an 'In Memoriam' that cited the Dutch fan meetings he attended. Rasa, Ray's first wife, was our guest in 2005.

The club's former board members are familiar names in Kinkdom: Huub Goudzwaard (who sadly died in 2023), Ruud Kerstiens, Siem van den Bergh, Rob Kopp and yours truly. Gerrit van den Berg supported us with wonderful publicity material. We had a lot of interactions with band members and, as John Dalton once put it, 'fans became friends.' Due to rising costs, the society was disbanded in 2014.

Van Veelen has published three books about the band in Dutch: *The Kinks: A Primal English Band* and two sequels covering concerts in the Netherlands and the solo careers of Ray and Dave Davies. He lives in Oosterbeek, The Netherlands.

1995
Steven Schindler – Fallbrook, California, US
The Kinks played the Hollywood House of Blues (no longer there) on 11 July 1995. At one point, about halfway through the show, Ray said, 'I didn't really want to play at the House of Blues, but now I don't think I ever want to play anywhere else! You're fantastic!' For the second encore, they played 'Days' in their usual subdued, emotional, sentimental fashion. I was standing off to the side, and I turned around to see English actress/comedian Tracey Ullman just behind me, sobbing uncontrollably during the entire song. I think the entire audience felt the same way. It was one of those unforgettable moments.

Ben Bolton – South Riding, Virginia, US
I have seen the Kinks live maybe a dozen times, mostly throughout the 1980s. I didn't really appreciate their music until *Low Budget* came out in 1979. I had heard of them prior to that but wasn't that familiar with their music except for the big hits like 'Lola', 'You Really Got Me' and so on. It wasn't until the early 1980s that I started seeing them live when they were a large-draw arena rock band. I'd seen them in numerous concert venues, usually the 10,000- to 20,000-seat sports arenas and outdoor concert venues. Those tours for *Give The People What They Want* and *State Of Confusion* were great, and I was still a relative newcomer as a Kinks fan. I was in my early 20s, and rock music was everything to me. (It still is, of course.)

My favourite show was on 17 July 1995 in Washington, DC. The Kinks played the now-closed Bayou. It was a smallish venue that held about 900 people but drew a lot of national acts. I had seen Graham Parker and The Ramones there, among others. I was very excited to see The Kinks in such an intimate setting. The Bayou had a pretty small stage with a small balcony section overlooking it. I sat in that balcony section. Ray opened the show with a short solo acoustic set before the rest of The Kinks joined him onstage for a full show. It was as amazing as I had hoped. I got to see my first Ray solo show, as well as my favourite band. (I wouldn't see another Ray solo show until over 20 years later during his *Other People's Lives* tour.) After the last encore, I reached over the railing as the band walked off the stage. Dave was pretty close to me, so I yelled, 'Dave!' He looked up and extended his hand. I leaned down and shook his hand, and as I did, he placed his pick into my palm. That was the best and, unfortunately, last Kinks show I ever saw.

The Kinks have brought me so much joy over the past few decades. I can never thank them enough for so much great music – and especially that Bayou show.

Mark Fucci – Stanley, Hong Kong, China
Our boys, aged 11 and 13, were getting through another rough summer. In July 1995, we managed to enjoy a nervous vacation at a lake in New Hampshire.

In the time before smartphones, the world often surprised you – with good news and bad. A local FM radio station announced that The Kinks would play nearby at Stratton Mountain Ski Resort in Vermont on Saturday night. Great news! We could see the show on the way home. Our children's first live rock concert! They were at an age when being seen in public with a parent was decidedly uncool, but The Kinks had been background music since birth, and I had been playing the *Phobia* album all summer. They both liked wonderful guitar riffs and harmonies on 'Still Searching'.

'They're pretty good. But why do you like them so much?'

'Fair question. It's not just the great melodies and musical talent. Their songs tell a story if you listen carefully.'

'What about?'

'Mostly things you first don't think are interesting: ordinary people living ordinary lives. The lyrics make fun of them, but then show respect for how they deal with life.'

'Huh?'

'Yeah, I know. You'll learn about irony soon enough. Just enjoy the music for now.'

We lucked into great seats – in the centre, maybe ten rows from the stage. Ray came out in a plaid flannel shirt and acoustic guitar. He did a short solo set that, in retrospect, was the beginning of his 'Storyteller' concept. Then the rest of the band joined, opening with a rousing 'Do It Again'. I had been to many Kinks concerts – I'd seen 'em low and seen 'em high. Never were the band tighter and more energised. The frenzy grew with each song. The crowd could not restrain themselves and they rushed the stage for the encore set.

'Dad!' said my oldest.

'Dad! We gotta go up there!' said my youngest.

'I don't know, it's ten deep. Not sure we can get close. Too crazy.'

'C'mon!'

'Screw it. You're right. Let's go!'

I put the younger boy on my shoulders. As we rushed forward, some divine hand opened a narrow gap in the gyrating mass, and we found ourselves directly below Dave. My boys bounced as wildly as the surrounding adults. Dave broke into the solo for 'You Really Got Me'. We caught his eye, and he reached down with his guitar so that my son could bang on the strings – just a few times before pulling away to work the rest of the crowd, now a wild mob. Amazing! Was it real or only a dream? The two-hour ride back to Hartford flew by, adrenaline pumping the entire trip.

The boy on my shoulders is now almost 40. He served as a Marine in Afghanistan and now lives on a beach in California. His brother lives in Denver with a wonderful wife and son. They look at me with exasperation when I tell them – yet again – that all of life's riddles are in a Kinks lyric. But whenever I talk about that night, they always smile.

Diane Germano – Watertown, Massachusetts, US

I initially encountered The Kinks' music during the British Invasion in the 1960s. Prior to that, my interest in rock music lagged behind the folk protest movement. All the British groups introduced a musical sensibility that resonated with me, moving the rock genre to the foreground. The Kinks were among my favourites.

Along with their peers, The Kinks performed their music on *Shindig!* and *Hullabaloo*. My sister and I sat glued to the television against our parents' strenuous protests against young men with long hair and go-go dancers in skimpy outfits. Additionally, the band received a great deal of airplay. My high school yearbook honoured 'A Well-Respected Man' on the list of songs that depicted our time.

I continued appreciating The Kinks' music through the decades: 'Come Dancing', 'Lola' and others. During my involvement in ballroom dancing in the early 1990s, I played 'Apeman' for the teacher and noted the sophistication and humour in the lyrics.

I did not attend rock concerts until the 1990s. The Kinks played the North Shore Music Theater in Beverly, Massachusetts, and the South Shore Music Circus in Cohasset, Massachusetts, during the summer of 1995. Ray opened the show in Beverly with: 'Who could open for The Kinks better than The Kinks?'

The show in Cohasset occurred in a sweltering tent, but the heat did not deter the band from delivering a superb show. In accordance with tradition, fans tossed paper plates onto the stage with song requests. Ray read some of them to the audience, with one telling him, 'We want to see your bum.' I was upset that Ray was being treated as an object rather than a human being. Those two concerts transitioned me from a casual fan to a diehard one.

I began writing letters to Ray after the shows in 1995. When he began touring with the 'Storyteller' shows, I attended my first concert at the Westbeth Theater in New York City. After that wonderful performance, I stood in line for Ray to autograph my copy of his 'unauthorised autobiography', *X-Ray*. After giving him my name so he could personalise his signature, he asked, 'What's your second name?' He had read my letters and has remembered my name since then.

The Westbeth show marked the beginning of my passion for photographing musicians. Ray granted permission to take pictures. I had merely wanted an image to commemorate the show, but something happened. To my amazement, I enjoyed the process of photographing Ray and other musicians. The passion has continued to this day. Thank you, Ray!

Paul Como – Massapequa Park, New York, US

I was born in 1955 and attended my first Kinks show in 1973 at the Palladium in New York City. I have been to about 50 Kinks shows, including Westbury, New York, in July 1995. Ray did a stellar solo performance at The Academy in New York City on 19 October 1995. Two days later, he appeared at

Shakespeare & Company Booksellers to do a reading from his book, *X-Ray*. I saw a flier at the show that he would be appearing at the bookstore. Another lifelong Kinks fan and friend of mine decided to take a chance. It paid off. We were among a crowd of about 200. Ray entered the room to cheers and flashbulbs from cameras. We were asked to please refrain from taking pictures during his reading. His Kinkdom gladly obliged. Photos were permitted after the readings. Ray read passages from *X-Ray*, along with some anecdotes. He periodically took questions from his fans. Midway through, I shouted: 'Ray, would you like a beer?' and he replied, 'Sure.' Out of my backpack came a beer in my Myrtle Beach cooler cup. My night was made! During the Q&A, I asked about 'Slum Kids'. He went into the story about why he would never play the song again. John Beecham, who was the trombone player with The Mike Cotton Sound, one day up and quit. He sent Ray a note thanking him for the posh hotels and good drugs, but he left the band. Ray responded to John, saying that he was an important member of the band, and due to his leaving, he would never perform 'Slum Kids' again.

Chris van Alem – Beers, The Netherlands

Fandom is not something you should just keep for yourself. Ever since I became a fan of The Kinks at age 13, I have done my best to spread their fame – with mixed results. Usually, I heard, 'Great stuff, The Kinks', and when asked, they said they had the *Greatest Hits* compilation. But hardly anyone could mention another album from their catalogue. It was hard to come across a soulmate.

My lucky day came in 1995. My second son, now 40 years old, was in grammar school in Nijmegen, the Netherlands. One day, he took a test in his English class, translating English words into their Dutch equivalent. One of the words was 'ceiling'. And yes, he knew what it meant. He wrote: 'This word reminds me of The Kinks song 'Dead End Street'. Do you happen to know The Kinks, sir?' The English teacher perked up, and he wondered: 'How does a 12-year-old kid in the 1990s know about a half-forgotten band from the 1960s?' 'It's my dad', my son told the teacher. 'He has been a Kinks fan since his youth.'

Within days, the connection between the teacher and me was made. We started talking about The Kinks, listening to The Kinks and visiting Dutch Kinks fan meetings. The teacher was very much into Ray's lyrics because his knowledge of English was far better than mine. He guided me through Ray's insights, pointed at phrases with double meanings and taught me how to put his songs into social perspective. I learned a lot, but I also should credit the English teacher from my own schooldays, who let me, in 1970, play parts of *Arthur* in his lessons and, together with the class, work out the meaning of 'Some Mother's Son'.

My son's teacher, René, didn't shy away from putting some Kinks stuff in his lessons. When young pupils came to the introduction days at his school, there always would be an important sentence on the blackboard of his classroom: 'Schooldays are the happiest days of your life', a quote from *Schoolboys In Disgrace*. The downside was that it took six years of hard work to discover whether it was true. The teacher was pleased to see that my eldest son put Ray's 'unauthorised autobiography', *X-Ray*, on his list for the compulsory exam in English literature.

Not long after the bond between René and me was established, thanks to the 'ceiling', our alliance was strengthened. The school's principal retired and, of course, got a successor. René would never conceal his love for The Kinks, not even in the staff room of the school, and the new principal noticed this. Time for his coming out: Ronald was a Kinks fan, too. The Nijmegen Kinks Trinity was established, and it exists to this day. From the day of his confession, Ronald will go through life being called The Headmaster. The three of us went to fan meetings in The Netherlands, visited London, gazed through the window of the Archway Tavern and marched up to Muswell Hill to visit The Clissold Arms. We were home. This was paradise, the place where the prophets of quintessential English pop music were born.

The Nijmegen Kinks Trinity will meet again soon. We will talk about each other's families, politics, football and The Kinks. Sometimes, we have a small Kinks quiz. It's my turn to put it together, and I will give them tough questions: Who sings this version of 'After The Ball'? Who is the guy who sings about knowing where Ray Davies lives? And who sings this snippet of 'Nobody's Fool'? Would you know the right answers? Let me know! If you get it right, we might invite you to join our Trinity, which then would become the Quintessential Quartet. On one condition, though: You gotta join in and sing along!

1996
Around The Dial With ... Kirk Madsen

In the 25 years I have spent in the concert business, I have witnessed how a number of performers have dealt with fame and fans. Some try their best to hide as much as possible. For example, Barry Manilow used to tour with a collapsible tunnel that would be set up from his dressing room to the stage. At the end of the show, it would be moved, so it went from the dressing room to his limo. This way, he could do a show and not have to encounter anyone. The other side of the coin would be David Lee Roth, who revelled in the adulation of his fans.

Most stars are like everyone else – they have good days and bad days where they just don't feel like dealing with people. When most people encounter a star, they feel that they may never have this opportunity again, so they take full advantage of it and will interrupt the star when they are eating or fighting with their wife or some other inappropriate time and then not understand why they are rebuffed.

Of all the performers I have worked with over the years, the one I know best is Ray Davies. I spent quite a bit of time with Ray. We got along well, and because I'm a fairly large guy, he liked having me close. Over time, in addition to all my other duties, I became something of a bodyguard. Ray would alternate between being comfortable with his fame and being bored with it. It was all he knew, having been a rock star since he was 18 years old. He would often say that making music was the important thing and not being famous, but I knew better.

Once when we were in Seattle (I think), we stayed in a hotel that had a restaurant and bar on the top floor. I was in my room relaxing when I got a call from Ray asking if I wanted to go to the bar. This was Ray's way of saying that he wanted to go to the bar and he wanted me next to him. I told him I would meet him in the hall by the elevator. We got on it and went up a floor when the door opened, and a very attractive young woman stepped in. Most people get into an elevator and turn around so they are facing the door, but this woman just stood there facing us. Ray was giving her his come-on smile. She looked at Ray and then looked at me and then looked at Ray again and then back to me. I think she did that three times before she looked at me, smiled and said, 'You look familiar. You're somebody famous, aren't you?' I didn't have to look at Ray to know what his expression was. It seemed as though the temperature in the elevator dropped about 20 degrees. The elevator door opened. As she got out, she asked if I was going to the bar. I said yes, and she said that if she came up there later, maybe she could get an autograph. I was trying very hard not to laugh out loud and said 'sure' as the door closed.

I thought this whole thing was hysterical, but obviously, Ray didn't. He just stood there staring forward until we reached our floor. The door opened, and I could see a few of the crew and Pete Mathison, Ray's guitar player, standing at the bar. I couldn't wait to tell them what happened. I stepped off the elevator and turned around in time to see Ray push the 'close door' button, and he was gone. He didn't speak to me (unless he had to) for two days. I never mentioned the incident in front of him again. I will tell you that the boys at the bar had a really good laugh, and the young woman never appeared for her autograph. I was going to sign it, Dave Davies. To paraphrase Oscar Wilde, 'The only thing worse than being noticed is not being noticed.'

Madsen has worked behind the scenes with many big-name acts, including tours with The Village People. He served as Ray Davies' stage manager and guitar tech from 1995 to 1998. He lives in Binghamton, New York.

Jerry Birenz – Belmar, New Jersey, US
How do Kinks songs affect or reflect my life? As so many others have said, they do in so many ways, from specific incidents to general themes. An example:

I moved, with my family, to a new house in February 1996. We had lived in our old house, our first house, for more than 15 years. Both of our daughters were born and raised there, and our careers started there. Fifteen years is a long time to live in one place – at the time, it was over a third of my life and half of my conscious life.

The street was a true neighbourhood, the kind that people dream about. We were good friends with many of our neighbours and knew all of them. We could all count on each other, from trivial things like borrowing milk or books to being able to trust each other with our children with no warning. We celebrated each other's happy events and mourned our losses. As far as I was concerned, I would live there forever. I never felt I had outgrown the house and never felt the urge for a change. I knew my children felt the same. (In fact, each of their best friends lived right next door.)

Unfortunately, my wife did not feel that way. Nothing against our neighbours, but she found her dream house and, yes, we moved. It was quite emotional for the girls and me, with one of my daughters crying uncontrollably and accusing us of betraying her. I felt torn out from my secure womb. Although we only moved to the next town, ten minutes from our old house, I felt very separate, very alone.

One day, six or eight weeks after we moved, in early spring, I swept leaves out of the garage while listening to *Fab Forty*, the collection of The Kinks' early singles, which I had just bought. On comes 'Autumn Almanac' and the following verse:

> This is my street, and I'm never gonna leave it
> And I'm always gonna stay here if I live to be 99
> 'Cause all the people I meet, seem to come from my street
> And I can't get away
> 'Cause it's calling me: Come on home
> Yes, it's calling me: Come on home...

I just stopped, I listened, I played it over and I started crying. I don't think I'll ever forget that moment when Ray provided me with a catharsis, letting all my pent-up emotions out by summarising, again, exactly how I feel about something important to me.

Marc Tulloch Hewson – Playa Flamenca, Alicante, Spain

Being born in 1962, I was a second-generation Kinks fan. I became aware of the band in 1978 when my younger sister bought a TV-advertised album titled *20 Golden Greats*. That was certainly true, with it featuring all the singles from 'You Really Got Me' to 'Apeman'. I duly taped it and wore out the cassette with repeated playings. I picked up a few Kinks albums along the way, and in 1987, I was sharing a house with my best friend, Neil. One day, in the *NME*, a piece about *The Village Green Preservation Society* hailed it as a lost classic but newly reissued. I told Neil about this and filed the information for the next time I hit a record shop. A day or so later, he came back from a trip into town and thrust a bag into my hands with the words: 'Happy birthday, Tulloch!' It was a brand-new copy of *Village Green*. I was gobsmacked, and we put the record on. It quickly became a firm favourite.

Scroll forward 18 years to the summer of 1996. My then-girlfriend (now wife) Catherine and I bought weekend tickets to the Cambridge Folk Festival. I noticed when we bought the programme that Ray Davies was playing solo on the last day of the festival in the penultimate slot before The Saw Doctors. To say I was excited was a massive understatement! Well, two days went by slowly, it seemed, and the intermittent showers didn't help. Finally, Sunday came, and we moved from our camp in the beer tent to a place with a good view of the stage. Ray came on with just an acoustic guitar, and the audience gave a huge cheer. Unfortunately, the skies darkened and spat forth heavy rain. The only dry places were onstage and in the beer tent. However, I wasn't going to miss Ray Davies for a drop of rain, and we stood our ground. He played an absolute blinder of a set, and the audience roared at the end of each song. We were kept entertained by Ray's between-song banter. The highlight was 'Sunny Afternoon' – in the pouring rain – and the entire audience singing along. By this time, happy tears ran down my cheeks and were washed away by the rain.

(Dedicated to my best friend and partner-in-crime, Neil John Hearfield. RIP, old mate)

1997
Around The Dial With ... Rob Bronstein

I first met Ray Davies in Seattle in the fall of 1996. I went to visit my oldest friend, who moved there in the 1980s, along with another close friend, Mike Konopka, who scored a job with Ray as his touring sound engineer. A few months earlier, Mike had called me saying that Ray and his tour manager, Bob Adcock, were unhappy with the lighting person they had, and Mike asked if I was interested. I thought it was a job with The Kinks, so I turned it down.

The vast majority of my lighting career had been with The Second City in Chicago. I had a 12-year run as their tour manager/stage manager before becoming the founding stage manager of The Second City e.t.c. space, a 180-seat cabaret. I had lit bands in my freshman year of college (1971-72) at the Mayfair branch of Chicago City College. I did not do that out of skill. I was the only person there that knew how to turn on the lighting board. I was afraid I wasn't up to lighting The Kinks and that I'd get hung out to dry by one of the idols of my youth. The first time I saw the band was on *Hullaballoo* or *Shindig!* at the age of 12 or so.

I timed my trip to Seattle to visit my old friend, see Mike and catch the show he was working on. It was *The Storyteller*, and as I watched, I realised I was born to do this show. I went out to dinner with them afterwards, and Ray sat across from me. We struck up a conversation and discovered that we were both fans of Peter Cook and Dudley Moore. I found out that Ray was a big fan of cabaret comedy and was a regular at The Second City improv set while he was doing *The Storyteller* in Chicago some months earlier. After dinner, I thought I was a lock for the lighting gig, but Ray's manager in London had already hired someone for the spring 1997 tour: Meic Hegget, a highly accomplished lighting designer and all-around nice guy.

In mid-March, I got a call from Bob at my home in Los Angeles. He told me there was an issue with Meic's work visa and he could not get into the US for the beginning of the tour, which started in the LA area. Would I be interested in doing a few shows, maybe a week? I leapt at the opportunity – but I had seen the show only once, six months before, as a patron. I was not studying the show. That night, I had consumed a few rounds and at least some herb. I had no script. Mike sent me an audio cassette of a recent performance and a playlist. I listened to it over and over, struggling to remember as much as I could. Mike wrote some notes on the playlist, doing his best to be helpful. The lighting guy sent me a plot and some patterns.

The first show was on 1 April in Irvine. The night before, Bob called again: 'Ray got in a little earlier than expected. Would you like to come to the hotel and see a videotape of the show?'

'Yes!'

'Oh, and since you're local, we don't have a room for you for tonight, so don't bring your satchel just yet.'

Irvine was 55 miles from my house. When I arrived, I found out that Ray had flown from London to New York, done radio interviews to support the tour and then got back on a plane and flew to LA. He was walking dead. In his room, Ray said 'hi' and 'nice to see you', then handed me his Sony Watchman, which had a screen of about three inches. The video was from a stationary camera at the back of the house from a show in Atlanta the previous fall, with Ray a quarter of an inch high on the three-inch screen.

I met with Mike and Kirk Madsen, who were Ray's stage manager and guitar tech, respectively. We watched the video together, and I furiously scribbled notes. It was a two-act piece with about 30 songs, and I got through the entire show once. I had to drive home and be back for a 10 am setup call. I took the Watchman and saw the first act again, but I was too tired and had to get up early for the 55-mile drive back to Irvine.

My girlfriend (at the time) drove me to the venue on April Fools' Day. I walked in to find four union electricians and a pile of lighting instruments on the stage.

One of them said: 'You the lighting designer?'

'Uh, yeah.' (Subtext: 'Sure, if you say so.')

'Where do we hang these?' he asked, gesturing to the instruments.

I shrugged, took out the plot and started reading it, trying not to look like I had no idea what I was doing.

At show time, I got through the first act with no issues, like I'd been doing it for months. About halfway through the second act, I blew a cue. Ray stopped talking and said, on the mic, 'Hey Rob, I'm over here!' Half of the audience turned and looked at the lighting booth. I was mortified.

After the show, I went to the dressing room and told Ray how sorry I was that I blew the cue. He laughed. 'I was just giving you some shit. You were fantastic! It's amazing you could just step in like that. You were great!'

I packed up the patterns and anything else I needed and went to the hotel, where we met for drinks. Ray stopped the chatter to offer a toast to me, saying to everyone present (the crew and a handful of fans who somehow knew where we were staying) that I did a great job. I completed six shows in six nights in five cities before Meic's visa was approved. A week with this legend who's in the Rock and Roll Hall of Fame.

In August, Bob called me again. Another band hired Meic, and he was unable to continue as Ray's lighting designer. Did I want to be the regular L.D.?

'Yes!'

I did three more tours and met the woman who would become my wife.

Bronstein is a writer, performer and voiceover artist who teaches theatre skills to at-risk teens in New York City, his current home. He served as Ray Davies' lighting designer from 1997 to 1998.

Geoff Lewis – Worcester, UK

Jim Smart is a Kinks fan from Honolulu who has had an enormous influence on my musical and Kinks-related life. Something good always seems to come out of our encounters. I first came across Jim in 1997. I had just joined Neil Ottenstein's Kinks Preservation Society – the daily KPS email digest was the main means of communication among fans around the world. Jim was a regular contributor. I spotted his Hawaiian email address and contacted him directly, mainly because I had lived in Honolulu for a year in the 1970s.

Jim had lots of interesting Kinks knowledge and many tracks that I had never even heard of. He often sent me tapes of these tracks to add to my collection. (Yes, technically, it was piracy, but I did buy the relevant albums as soon as they became available again!) In one communication, he mentioned an interest in the places that crop up in Kinks songs – for example, he spotted Praed Street in Paddington on a visit to London. As a former London resident, I already knew a lot of the locations, and I suggested that we collaborate on a website dedicated to the Kinks' London. The Big Black Smoke website was born.

Later that year, Jim visited the UK. I invited him to my Worcester home and suggested we set up a scratch band to play in my local pub, the Dragon. He agreed, and I gathered a group of local musician friends for the occasion. After I had obtained an agreement from the landlady of the Dragon, Jim got cold feet and said he would rather not do it. However, I was now committed and felt the gig had to go ahead anyway. When Jim heard this, he relented and said he would play. Unfortunately, by this time, I had already named the band Jim Chickens Out. Luckily, Jim has a good sense of humour. The gig was a roaring success – not all Kinks songs, but the set included a good selection of them. The band carried on playing very popular gigs, without Jim, for the next 20 years as The Fingers.

Early in 1998, a girlfriend asked me to find out about the rumoured songwriting courses that Ray Davies taught, as she really wanted to go on one. I did some research and got details of the Arvon Foundation, which I also made known on the KPS digest. Shortly afterwards, I received an email from Jim telling me that he had applied and been accepted, and he suggested I do the same. Of course, I did, and we met at Ray's course in Devon that March. It was a truly wonderful week spent with a great bunch of folks. Ray was really great, too, although he made us work hard. It was here that I first met Olga Ruocco, someone who was to become another major Kinks kollaborator. My girlfriend never did go on the course, but she met Ray later that year when we went to his gig in Santa Rosa, Calif. – he had invited me to meet up with him afterwards.

Some time passed until I next met Jim when he visited the UK again in 2010. We performed a short Jim Chickens Out reunion at the Marr's Bar in Worcester, then went to London together. He had an ambition to play at the Clissold Arms, the spiritual home of The Kinks in Muswell Hill. We went along there on a Friday evening and asked George Karageorgis – who had recently taken over the place – if it would be okay to play a few Kinks songs.

George had a more enlightened view of the Kinks connection than the previous owners, who had removed almost all the memorabilia that had been there when fans gathered for a Kinks singalong (usually with me playing keyboards and occasionally someone on acoustic guitar). He agreed, so Jim got out his guitar, I got out my keyboard and we jammed a few Kinks classics. To our delight, the Crouch End Festival Chorus, who were working with Ray at that time, were in the bar having an after-rehearsal meal, and they sang along. Huge fun!

George really enjoyed it, so I asked him if we could bring the annual Kinks singalong back to the Clissold after being exiled to other pubs for several years. George said we could if we waited until the diners had finished eating. A few weeks later, I took my keyboard along, the fans congregated and we had a fun night singing Kinks songs. It went down so well that George wanted it to become an annual event. This, of course, led to the formation of the Kinksfan Kollektiv, a band of musicians from around the world who play in London every year.

Jim has been over twice since then – in 2015, he joined members of the Kinksfan Kollektiv for an 'unplugged' Kinks Night at the Clissold, and in 2022, he joined the full KFK for gigs at the Clissold and the Springfield in Bounds Green. This was intended to extend to gigs in the Netherlands, but sadly, COVID-19 got in the way.

Jim saw videos of the KFK performing in July 2023, which included Dave Davies as an enthusiastic member of the audience. He says this made him very jealous, and he is aiming to come again in 2024! I am looking forward to it.

See the Big Black Smoke website at *london.kastoffkinks.co.uk/html/big_black_smoke.html*.

Leslie Ohanian – Ann Arbor, Michigan, US

My Kinks fan journey started when I was nine and my older brother brought home a copy of *Lola Versus Powerman And The Moneygoround*. I heard 'Lola' on the radio and loved it, but as I listened to the LP further, the song 'Strangers' caught my ear and heart. Every birthday and Christmas or any gift-giving occasion after that, my brother would get me another Kinks LP. I'm pretty sure he lived to regret it when he got me *Word Of Mouth* and I played 'Living On A Thin Line' repeatedly. I always seemed to be drawn to Dave's songs – they spoke to me most of all.

Fast-forward to 1997. When Dave Davies announced his first solo tour, one of the dates was in a city nearby. I had just started dating my (now) husband, Fritz, and he offered to buy tickets and get us to the venue to see the show. My heart sank when the concert was cancelled. Fritz, seeing how devastated I was, hatched a plan to get us to the show in Chicago at the House of Blues. So, we embarked on our first road trip as a couple. The show was even better than I would have imagined. Dave shone as a frontman, and the crowd loved him.

As a longtime concert-goer and a veteran of a few Kinks shows, I had never actually queued up afterwards to get an autograph – but that night, clutching my copy of Dave's autobiography, *Kink*, I waited. Even as I stood there, I knew it might be in vain, but I had to try. Moments later, someone stepped in front of me. My brain took far too long to realise the smiling man was Dave himself. He chuckled and said, 'I can't sign the book if you don't let go of it …' and gently took it from me. I stammered something about really enjoying the show and how good he was, to which he laughed and teasingly called me a liar and that he appreciated it. Before I could say anything else, Dave hugged me and handed me back the book, and then he moved to the next waiting fan.

Joanne Corsano – Bourne, Massachusetts, US

I first saw The Kinks in concert on 3 June 1978 at the Providence (Rhode Island) Civic Center. Ray was very 'on' as the frontman, and Dave and Jim Rodford had a blast doing synchronised dance steps as they expertly played their instruments. What impressed me the most was the other fans. Everyone seemed to know all the words to all the songs, even the deep cuts that I never heard on the radio. I left that show with a real appreciation for the joy that comes with being a Kinks fan.

I was off to the Harvard Coop to buy a couple of their recent LPs and a greatest hits compilation or two, and over the next few years, I attended several more concerts. At the show at the Cape Cod Melody Tent on 27 July 1995, no one (except maybe Ray) knew that this was The Kinks' farewell tour. At that concert, I gained a new appreciation for Dave. He was hot as ever on the guitar, sang three lead vocals, and, most of all, seemed to be really enjoying himself. Not only did I struggle to see any of the legendary animosity between Ray and Dave but Dave was giving admiring glances toward Ray.

That was around the time that the internet was taking hold. I joined the mailing list maintained by Neil Ottenstein (later named the Kinks Preservation Society) and also the discussion group alt.fan.kinks on Usenet. Having these places to talk about the band fuelled my enthusiasm for their music, and I started to form online friendships.

The first Kinks fan I met in person was Jill Brand (later to become legendary for cooking Indian meals for Dave when he played at the Sit 'n' Bull Pub in Boston's suburbs). I got chummy with Leslie Ohanian, a Michigan resident, because she shared my interest in Dave's music.

In 1996 and early 1997, I saw Ray Davies perform solo a half-dozen times, and the Kinkdom buzzed with the big question: are The Kinks done as a band? It was obvious that Dave was asking himself this same question because, in the spring of 1997, he assembled a band of musicians in Los Angeles and performed a handful of solo shows. I regret that I didn't drop everything and fly to LA to see his first-ever solo show, but I did see him on 19 November in Cleveland, Ohio, with my new friends Leslie and Fritz. That was the first of 54 solo shows by the Dave Davies Band that I saw between 1997 and 2003.

I will forever honour the memory of the two number-one Dave fans, Rafaela Filippi and Frank Reda, who each saw Dave over 100 times and were intensely loyal to him. I spent many happy hours waiting in line with them to get into venues and talking about music and shows we'd seen. They both have departed this earthly plane but will never be forgotten.

Around The Dial With … Dave Nolte

My earliest memories of hearing The Kinks are courtesy of my oldest brother and his friends hanging out and playing records. 'Victoria' was the first song that really stuck out among everything they would listen to. *The Kinks Kronikles*, courtesy of another brother, was the next step and made me a lifelong fan.

Jumping ahead a couple of decades, I got to work with Dave Davies on his first solo tour as his roadie/guitar tech courtesy of my friends in his band. This led to recording with him, getting a spot in his band (while still serving as his guitar tech) and touring with him.

One of the first tours I did as a musician with him included a show at the Bottom Line in New York City. I had met and gotten to know many of the diehard Kinks fans at this point, and one of them let me know that Pete Quaife was in town and was coming to the show. It was tricky because they wanted to surprise Dave, but Dave doesn't like surprises. We had it set up before the show that I would walk Pete back to see Dave. So, I'm super-excited, waiting in a hallway, when Pete rounds the corner and says, 'Who the fuck are you?'

Dave was very happy to see Pete and invited him up to play 'You Really Got Me' with us at the end of the night. I was onstage with half of The Kinks! I later found out Pete was in town to see Dave and Ray separately to see about playing together again. I wish it had happened.

Fast-forward another decade, and I was on tour travelling from London to Cork, Ireland. The queue to get on the plane was a free-for-all, with everyone in the room moving toward one doorway. Just as I make it to the door, I look up to see Ray and his companion standing there. I had a flood of thoughts about what to say but ended up telling them they could go first. Ray looked at me suspiciously, then said, 'Thanks, man.'

That was amazing – I was blown away by the encounter. Looking back, I think Ray and I were the only people to check a bag when we landed, as it was just the two of us at the carousel. It took a few minutes for the bags to show up, and I sat there telling myself to go talk to him, then telling myself not to bother him. I thought, 'Just tell him you play with his brother.' I then thought maybe he wouldn't like that, so why not just tell him how much his music meant to me? Again, I talked myself out of it. My encounter with him was enough, so I decided not to push my luck.

I consider myself very lucky to have played with Dave for so long and to have met Pete and Ray. Mick Avory, I'm looking for you!

Nolte toured and performed with Dave Davies from 1997 to 2019. He lives in Hermosa Beach, California, US.

1998
Mitch Friedman – Red Bank, New Jersey, US
During the first week of March 1998, I made my way with 15 other intrepid souls to the village of Sheepwash in Devon, UK, to attend Ray's annual songwriting workshop. We were all nervous, but probably none more so than me because I couldn't even perform one of my own songs on acoustic guitar the whole way through without making sloppy mistakes.

Over the next six days, through a series of thought-provoking assignments built around either writing as or for someone else, I toiled away and slowly gained newfound confidence. For the final task, Ray had us write and perform *Thelma & Louise: The Musical*, with each student assigned a character from the film and a song or two to advance the storyline. I was cast as the Harvey Keitel detective who was hoping to crack his first big case after years of struggling to make a name for himself on the police force.

Secure I'd written my best song of the week, titled 'Crack The Case', I played it for Ray to provide feedback hours before the class performance. He jumped up at the end and gave me a standing ovation. 'That's fucking great, Mitch!' I'd intentionally whipped up a chorus that had a vaguely Kinks-esque sound, with a chunky power chord riff and the words 'I will crack the case … alone! I will crack the case!'

When it was my turn to sing my little ditty during the musical, everyone chuckled upon hearing the first chorus. The moment I let the final chord ring out, Ray quickly clapped and then caught himself because we were told to hold all applause until the show's end. This made us all laugh, and I was very proud. At the end of the show, Ray called out to me, 'Mitch, sing your chorus!' – which I did twice because Ray told me to keep going as everyone, including him, sang along. It was the best feeling of my life.

In August 2000, I was waiting in line outside the Jane Street Theatre in Greenwich Village to see Ray try out some new songs with Yo La Tengo backing him. As he made his way past us, he recognised me. 'Hey, Mitch. Good to see you again, mate! I will crack the case … alone! I will crack the case!' Nearly three years later, he remembered the chorus to one of my songs. It thrilled me to no end.

Five years after that, my friend Dave Gregory, formerly of XTC, auditioned to replace Mark Johns in Ray's solo touring band. Dave casually dropped my name, and Ray instantly sang, 'I will crack the case … alone! I will crack the case!' Despite having taught seven intervening workshops since the one I attended, he still recalled my chorus. What an incredible honour, considering I've had a few hundred of his fantastic choruses going through my head since 1979!

Friedman has written four books and 2022's *Swell Goatee: My Life In The Hair After* includes a chapter with the full story about his experiences at Ray's songwriting workshop.

Chris Locke – Dartmouth, Massachusetts, US

I bought my first Kinks album in 1976 – the *File Series*. I was a mere eight years old, handed ten bucks and sent into the record store (the 'babysitter' of the era) by my mother as she went to shop elsewhere. I had never heard of The Kinks before, but KISS were one of my first favourite bands, so I will guess that I was browsing the 'KISS' section on the record rack when I saw 'KINKS' in front of it. Pure happenstance.

The *File Series* record captured my attention just by reading the song titles themselves. It surely wasn't its bland and basic album cover (it's no *Low Budget* album art!). I played those records (it was a double album) over and over on a briefcase-style children's record player, connecting with, learning and loving every single song. A new Kinks fan was born! I still have the same LPs nearly 50 years later, though they're also the most warped and scratched records in my moderate-sized collection and complemented years ago with a mint copy.

The Kinks were always my number-one band from then on, struggling sometimes to maintain that spot through my experiences with The Beatles, Led Zeppelin, Kiss, Pink Floyd, Van Halen and a few others through the years, but always prevailing in the end. Then, decades later, along came the internet with its bulletin boards and mailing lists, including Neil Ottenstein's email list. I was thrilled to finally find a significant number of fellow Kinks fans who appreciated their music.

After years of sharing experiences, stories and all things Kinks-related with these new friends and fans of the band, we talked about making ourselves an official 'fan club', for lack of a better term. This was probably back in 1996-97. We decided we should choose a name and make T-shirts that we could all wear to the upcoming Ray and Dave solo shows. As a graphic/web designer, I was fortunate to design the tee, and the Kinks Preservation Society was born.

I don't think I had even met any fellow KPSers yet, and one day in 1998, I received an email that was curious to me but also made me suspicious. It read something like, 'Hi Chris, my name is Christian, Dave Davies' son, and we were wondering if you'd be interested in helping us build a website for Dave.' I responded but, again, felt wary. I mentioned that in the email, and Christian asked me to send him a KPS T-shirt. A week later, he sent me another email with a photo attachment of Dave wearing our beloved KPS shirt to help rest my identity concerns, and it did!

We got to work on building his site, and I was a very proud Kinks fan, given the opportunity to help Dave keep his fans involved with his musical and spiritual aspirations. We even did a 'webcast' back in the day, hosted at the now-infamous Sit 'n' Bull Pub in Maynard, Massachusetts, with the help of Peter Bochner and others.

In addition to all the great people I became friends with over those years of Ray and Dave solo tours, I like to think that Dave and I also became friends while working together. I'll never forget him calling my wife and me to congratulate us on the birth of our third child, Angela Christine. He is an honourable, thoughtful, sweet and kind man, and I'll always remember those great years of my life very well, thanks to him and many of you.

Alfred Russell – Halfweg, The Netherlands

Imagine this: It seems like an ordinary workday, but before you know it, you find yourself in a luxury hotel suite sitting across from Ray Davies! This happened to me in the early spring of 1998. I was working for *Haarlems Dagblad*, a regional newspaper in the Netherlands that is often said to be the world's oldest continuously published newspaper. I visited businesses to sell them advertising space. It wasn't that difficult because the internet had not yet replaced print media. I spent most of my workdays cruising around in a company car, always with music playing, especially The Kinks. Everyone around me knew they were my favourite band.

That morning, as I walked down the hallway in the main office, someone yelled out loudly, 'KINKS!' I turned around, and there was John Oomkes, the editor-in-chief of the arts section, walking toward me. I'll never forget the words he spoke: 'I'm going to interview Ray Davies – do you want to come along?' Of course, I wanted to come along! I dropped my work, and together, we drove to Amsterdam, where Ray was going to meet the press to promote his upcoming *Storyteller* tour. Journalists from various media outlets gathered at the beautiful Hotel Americain and each was granted a one-on-one interview with Ray in a suite on the first floor. When it was our turn to go upstairs, Ray waited for us at the doorway, saying, 'Hi guys, come in …' I could hardly believe it. Was this really happening?

We took our seats, John conducted the interview, and I was a silent witness, eagerly absorbing all the impressions. The interview went incredibly well, especially because John, who had interviewed many celebrities before, didn't ask Ray the usual clichéd questions. When a tray of coffee was brought in, I poured Ray's coffee for him. I thought it should have been tea!

A month later, I met Ray again thanks to fellow fan Tracy Noonan, with whom I had travelled to Cologne for a *Storyteller* show. Afterwards, we sat in the lounge of the Renaissance Hotel with Ray, Pete Matheson and the German documentary filmmaker Sigrid Faltin, who claimed she wanted to make a film about Ray. When a waiter came to take our drink orders, Ray asked if they had cigars. They didn't, so I offered Ray a cigarette, which he smoked halfway and then handed back to me to put out in the ashtray next to me.

'Where have we met before?' he asked.

'Well, I was the guy who served you coffee last month!'

Brad Toussaint – Redwood City, California, US

After Ray's 21 May 1998 show at the King Kat Theatre in Seattle, I waited with a crowd for him to emerge and sign autographs. I realised I stood next to local Pacific Northwest music legend Scott McCaughey, who, with R.E.M.'s Peter Buck, had joined Ray on stage for a song or two. He graciously chatted with me, confirming his reputation as a great guy. I asked for his autograph, but all I had was a copy of the *Village Green Preservation Society* album. Scott said, 'I can't sign someone else's album!' I am not sure what I told him to change his mind, but he relented, signing it: 'To Brad, a fellow Kinks lover …' Pretty awesome. It put Scott's band's name, Young Fresh Fellows, in a new light. A Kinks-loving fellowship.

One of the ways I discover new bands to check out is when I hear that band members are Kinks fans. The only reason I let my wife convince me to watch *The Queen's Gambit* is because I found out the lead actress, Anya Taylor-Joy, loves the band. I have spent most of my adult life desperately seeking fellow Kinks lovers.

Fast-forward to 2002. Still in Seattle, this time at the annual Labor Day weekend Bumbershoot festival. Besides the thrill of seeing Dave perform that weekend, I was excited to see another favourite, Wilco, which I had discovered because of their reported appreciation of The Kinks, including covering 'Oklahoma USA' in their early days. I read, I think in *Rolling Stone*, that Wilco would launch into '20th Century Man' during soundchecks, too.

Wilco's *Yankee Hotel Foxtrot* had come out recently, so I had a copy for them to autograph in their meet-and-greet after their set. With my wife and six- and four-year-old boys (all fellow Kinks lovers, even back then), we had a nice chat with Jeff Tweedy. I brought up The Kinks, and he confessed his fandom. I asked if he could sign the album to a fellow Kinks lover. He enthusiastically obliged.

The next year, The Thorns (Matthew Sweet, Shawn Mullins, and Pete Droge) opened for another Kinks-loving band, The Jayhawks, at the Moore Theater. Both bands were awesome. The Thorns signed autographs at their merch table during the intermission. Having heard that Matthew Sweet was a fellow Kinks lover, I was hoping for a Jeff Tweedy-type response to my now-routine request. Matthew looked at me like I was crazy (not necessarily an unreasoned response but lacking the enthusiasm I anticipated), but he did agree about The Kinks and obliged.

I've had mixed luck with other artists' responses over the years. Jonathan Richman, for example, just kind of gave me a side-eyed, suspicious grin and signed his name. That seems about right. I'm still working on getting others like Gary Louris of The Jayhawks. Most importantly, though, I'm still on the hunt for newer Kinks-loving bands – the young, fresh fellow Kinks lovers!

Around The Dial With ... Tom Kitts

In May 1998, friend and fellow Kinks aficionado Mike Kraus and his wife, Linda, took a circuitous route from Wisconsin to my Brooklyn home. They drove through Canada, stopping in Belleville (just outside of Toronto) to pick up another house guest, Peter Quaife. Pete and I had corresponded but never met. He was not coming to see me, though. There were three shows that weekend that he was anxious to attend: Dave Davies on 23 May at New York's legendary Bottom Line, Ray Davies on 24 May in Atlantic City and Ray (again) on Memorial Day evening in East Hampton, Long Island.

Mike let a few Kinks fans know that Pete would be at the Bottom Line show. As soon as we arrived, fans approached Pete, expressed appreciation for his work and asked for autographs. This continued as we took our table in the club. Pete was overjoyed. At one point, he noticed Billy J. Kramer near the bar. 'I thought you were dead', Pete quipped. Kramer did not miss a beat: 'No, I thought you were dead.' They shared a few memories as they awaited Dave's appearance. Throughout the performance, fans called for Dave to invite Pete to the stage. Dave ignored them. Pete whispered to me that Dave still held a grudge against him for leaving the Kinks 30 years previously.

Finally, for the encore, Dave invited Pete on stage. Pete hustled as if afraid Dave would retract the invitation. Dave Jenkins graciously yielded his bass, and the band blasted into 'You Really Got Me' to deafening applause. I asked Pete what he thought of his old bandmate's performance. 'He got a whole lot better, that's for sure.' I didn't know if he was joking.

The following night in Atlantic City, Mike, Linda, Pete and I sat at the hotel bar near the entrance to the theatre. At one point, we spotted Ray and approached him. 'Crutch', Ray greeted his former bandmate with his famed lopsided smile. After some small talk, Ray exited to prepare for the show. During the performance, Ray asked Crutch to take a bow. Curiously, Ray dropped a passage or two in which he discussed the early days with Pete. By this point, I had seen *20th Century Man* several times. I don't remember anything that Pete would have found offensive. Ray dropped the same passages the next night, too.

The East Hampton show was a fundraiser with expensive tickets. Ray's secretary back in London arranged for two – but only two – complimentary tickets for Pete and me. Mike and Linda graciously volunteered to remain in Brooklyn. The weather was terrible that Memorial Day, rainy and chilly, so Pete and I gave ourselves plenty of time for the drive. We entered the theatre two or three hours before showtime. We planned to talk to Ray and then get something to eat.

We entered the simply decorated but elegant theatre. Pete and I were not, let's say, dressed for a fundraiser in the Hamptons. Pete, far removed from his fashionable days as a Mod, had on an unstylish blue windbreaker and a pair of jeans, and I was certainly no more stylish than Pete. A young woman, probably in her late 20s, staffed the counter. She wore sparkling earrings and a matching bracelet with what was, no doubt, a very expensive dress. I inquired about our tickets. The conversation went something like this:

'Your name?'

'Kitts.'

She looked at the list and, without looking up, said, 'No, I don't see anything.'

Peter started with his quips. 'You know, he's a doctor or professor. Maybe you should look under that.'

'Well, can you check with Bob Adcock, Ray Davies's road manager?' I asked.

'No.'

'Maybe you can ask your supervisor. I'm with Peter Quaife. He was in The Kinks with Ray. Maybe the tickets are under his name.'

Pete added: 'I do a good English accent, so I must've been in his band, right?'

Unimpressed, she sought out her supervisor.

'Let me handle this,' I told Pete, whose restless wit had a lifetime propensity of exerting itself at inopportune times.

The young woman informed us that 'the performer' had been delayed. We asked her to recommend a restaurant. With her best haughtiness and disdain, she sneered, 'There's a tavern down the street that serves hamburgers.'

As we left, I asked Pete if she was as obnoxious as I thought. He agreed. We were in the Hamptons, high season was just underway, and there were all kinds of fabulous restaurants nearby.

'But that bar sounds good, doesn't it?' Pete said.

'Yeah. Let's go.'

When we returned, the lobby was crowded. I approached the counter and asked our friend about our tickets. Her supervisor, also elegantly dressed, heard our inquiry and interrupted: 'Mr. Davies has been delayed. His flight from Philadelphia was cancelled, but he is driving and should arrive shortly.' We went outside just as Ray and his road manager, Bob, pulled into the entrance behind the hall. We talked to Ray for a few minutes, but he was anxious to get to the dressing room to prepare for his performance in about 30 minutes. Bob assured us he would take care of our ticket situation.

We returned to our young friend. She glared at us, but before we could say anything, her supervisor smiled and – I'm not making this up – said, 'Oh, Mr. Quaife and Dr. Kitts, we have your tickets.' We got the last laugh. She instructed the young woman to escort us to our fourth-row seats. The young woman, who could not muster a smile at us, did not say anything, not even a begrudging 'enjoy the show.'

I told Pete that I had never experienced snobbery like that. 'I have,' he replied. When he tried to check in at the Waldorf Astoria Hotel for the Rock and Roll Hall of Fame induction ceremony in 1990, they could not find his room. The front desk clerk treated him like a fraud. However, after waiting for some time in the lobby, the same clerk approached Pete to apologise, informing him and his wife that it was an oversight and that his room was ready. He recalled that moment fondly.

After that weekend, Pete and I communicated frequently. He was a great resource for my book on Ray, and I served as an editor on *Veritas,* his wonderful rock 'n' roll novel. (To be honest, *Veritas* did not need much editing. Pete was a skilled writer.) More personally, we supported each other through our divorces. Pete always knew what to say.

In the summer of 2008, my future wife, Lisa, and I stayed at his and his partner's home in Copenhagen. It was an incredible experience with Pete and Elisabeth. My favourite memory from that trip was a 'Christmas in July' celebration, complete with Pete singing Danish folksongs, an elaborate smorgasbord with traditional Danish foods and many shots of schnapps. But that's a story for another day.

Kitts, a professor of English at St. John's University, is the author of *Ray Davies: Not Like Everybody Else* and co-editor (with Mike Kraus) of *Living On A Thin Line: Crossing Aesthetic Borders With The Kinks*. He lives in Brooklyn, New York, US.

Peter Bochner – Wayland, Massachusetts, US

I became a co-owner of the Sit 'n' Bull Pub in Maynard, Massachusetts, after my friend from Boston University, Ted Epstein, returned to the area to manage a dive bar and invited me to invest. Who could say no to owning a bar? (Answer: A prudent human being with a brain. Unfortunately, I wasn't one of those.)

On 1 December 1997, I went with three other Kinks fans – Barry Mooney, Lew Blatt and Martin Greissmer – to see Dave Davies at the Met Café in Providence, Rhode Island. After the show, I got the name of the person who handled Dave's booking from a member of his entourage. Months later, when I read that Dave would hit the road again, I dug up the name and asked Ted if he'd be interested in booking Dave. Ted thought it would be a big risk for our small club. I said, 'I guarantee at least 75 people will come', and promised that I would personally underwrite some of the cost of the show in exchange for a piece of the profits – if there were any. So, Ted started the negotiations. To help meet Dave's guarantee, we said we'd give him a $100 bonus for playing 'Mindless Child Of Motherhood' (my idea, obviously). The wrangling went on and on, and then, one day, Ted called me. 'Pete, get ready. We booked Dave. Thursday, June 4.'

We publicised the show on the Kinks Preservation Society email list, and I sent an exclusive announcement to the *Boston Globe* because I knew their chief music writer, Jim Sullivan, was a big Kinks fan. Our 160-capacity club sold out almost overnight. Dave's schedule precluded adding a second show on the following night, but his agent suggested doing two shows on 4 June. We agreed, and the late show sold out as well. We moved up the start time for the first show to 7:30 pm, with the second show at 10 pm. But the story about how close that show – and likely all subsequent Dave shows at the Bull – came to not happening has never been told before.

The 4 June show arrived. Dave's soundcheck was scheduled for 2 pm. I worked a half-day and drove to the Bull, which was about 20 minutes from my house. When I got there, at around 1:30, nine fans were already there, a few of whom I knew. We started bonding. We kept an eye out for Dave's bus. When it hadn't shown up by 3:45, I feared that the band had gotten lost or had the wrong day. At 4 pm, a tour bus pulled into the parking lot across the street. Dave, his three band members and his road manager entered the Bull to applause from the fans. Dave looked regal in a cloak that brought back images of early Kinks album covers. We all met, and he asked us to clear the room so the band could start its soundcheck. We told the fans to go outside – they could listen but not watch. I was allowed to stay because I was a Bull employee.

Dave started by playing the opening riff of 'You Really Got Me'. It was ear-shattering, its loudness amplified by the emptiness of the barroom. I felt my insides vibrating. At one point, the band launched into The Beatles' 'I Wanna Hold Your Hand', with Dave changing the words to 'I don't know where I am', probably because he didn't – we were the last stop on his tour.

A few songs into the soundcheck, Dave's road manager, Rich Rees, approached Ted and asked if he had checked Dave's rider. When Ted said he had, Rees asked why we had the wrong amp. Ted said the rider called for a Marshall amp. Rees said it was the wrong Marshall. Ted asked if that was a problem, and Rees said, 'It's a *big* problem. Dave won't play without the right amp.'

The Bull had two phone lines. I got on one, Ted got on the other. We started calling local music stores to find the right Marshall. It was after 5 pm, and some were closed for the day. Luckily, Guitar Center in Natick had one they'd rent to us, but we would have to pick it up. Natick is three towns over from Maynard, which is normally a half-hour ride. But this was rush hour, and the only way to get there was Route 27, a two-lane road that would be jammed with commuters. I jumped in my car and, breaking every traffic law, made it to Guitar Center in 50 minutes. I spent another 15 minutes signing out the amp and putting it in my car, then raced back to the Bull. By the time I made it back, it was 7 pm and the club was packed with fans, all unaware of how close the show came to not happening. Ted let Dave know his Marshall was there, and I went to the bar for a much-needed drink. I won't describe the show itself. You can read fan Joanne Corsano's excellent review at nicepace.net/concerts/1999/19980604davedavies.htm

Between shows, Rees asked if I was serious about paying $100 to hear 'Mindless Child Of Motherhood'. I said, 'Hell yeah.' But at 12:45, 15 minutes before the club was supposed to close, it hadn't been played. Just as I thought, 'At least I'll save $100', the band launched into the tune. At that point, the combination of emotion and whatever I was drinking carried me onstage, uninvited, and I sang the chorus of the song into bass player Dave Jenkins' mic. He didn't seem to mind.

The next day, the *Boston Globe* published Jim Sullivan's glowing review of the show. In it, he wrote, 'Sit 'n' Bull co-owner/MC/Kinks nut Peter Bochner was in heaven, calling it 'my proudest moment as a club owner.'' And that was the start of the relationship between Dave and the Bull that would span 15 more shows.

René Smits – Uden, The Netherlands
I became a Kinks fan in 1965 when I was ten years old. My first single was 'Dedicated Follower Of Fashion'. I have two older brothers – one loved The Animals, the other brother The Beatles. I also wanted to have a favourite pop group, so I chose The Kinks. Since that time, I collected everything about The Kinks from Dutch newspapers and the music press. (Today, I have six scrapbooks filled with clippings!)

In November 1998, I visited London for the annual Kinks Fan Club meeting at the Archway Tavern – my second visit, and again, I was very impressed by all those Kinks fans from all over the world. I spoke to Mick Avory and asked him if it were possible to visit Konk Studios. He said, 'No chance – you have to make an appointment. But I am in the studio at midday Monday, so you can come then.' Unfortunately, my plane back to Amsterdam was scheduled for 3 pm.

On Monday morning, I left my hotel in Muswell Hill and went searching for Konk Studios on Tottenham Lane. After taking pictures, I rang the bell with no hope of going in. After the fourth ring, somebody asked me who I was, so I told her I spoke to Mick Avory, who said I could visit the studio. She said, 'Of course, come in, please.' She was the cleaning woman, and she thought that I was a musician! She showed me everything in the studio, and I was so impressed that I thought, 'This can't be true. René Smits is now in the heart of The Kinks!' Unbelievable. All those instruments, guitars, mixing consoles, digital tape desks, monitors and so on. After taking pictures, she offered me a very nice cup of coffee in the basement, where there was a billiard room. I knew it from the picture in the Velvel CD reissue of *Misfits*. Fantastic!

Then, the cleaning woman asked me if I knew the studio manager. I said I knew her name but didn't know her personally. The cleaning woman phoned her, and the manager wasn't happy to hear that an unknown guy from Holland was there. I got on the phone and told her about the Kinks meeting at the Archway and that I had spoken to Mick. She asked me to leave the building immediately and come back another time after making an appointment. I finished my coffee and said goodbye to the cleaning woman, thanking her very, very, very much for letting me in.

It was a very special Kinks weekend in London that I never will forget.

Around The Dial With ... David Temple MBE

When Ray and I first met in late summer 1998, Ray was 54 and I was 44, which doesn't seem so far apart at all, but my first experience of The Kinks was in 1964 when Ray was 20 and I was ten! In those days, the famous bands all had their own monthly magazines, and I became engrossed in the Davies siblings and their songs.

Moving forward to 1998, out of the blue, Ray telephoned my house when I was out. My wife said he would ring back. 'Hello, is that David Temple? My name is Ray Davies – I'm not sure if you've heard of me?' 'Er ... yes ...' I stuttered, unable to speak! Ray was writing a choral work for the Norfolk and Norwich Festival, and he wanted my advice about writing for choirs. It turned out that I was asked to direct the chorus in rehearsals for Ray's piece 'The Flatlands', and there began a musical and personal relationship that lasts to this day.

For this project, Ray was very 'hands-on' and recorded all my rehearsals so he could monitor the project. I was unable to attend the world premiere, but I did hear the second performance in Chelmsford a month or so later. I then sent a letter to Ray with some thoughts on his piece, and all went quiet. It must have been at least a year later that my wife and I bumped into him in Highgate – and, miraculously, he picked out my letter from his back pocket. We chatted about the work and began to cement a friendship. I helped with a small recording project for him a year or two later, and we met socially on occasion.

The next big event in our collaborations came from a pub conversation after a Crouch End Festival Chorus concert that Ray had attended. He told me that the BBC had asked him to take part in their Electric Proms at London's Roundhouse later that year (2007), and he had the idea of including my choir in that. The concert was a great success, and it was particularly memorable for the arrangement (by Steve Markwick) of 'Shangri-la'.

Very soon afterwards, Ray came to my house for Sunday lunch, and we discussed the idea of further shows throughout the UK and the possibility of a new album to be called *The Kinks Choral Collection*. Once all was signed and sealed, the album was recorded in Konk Studios (the band and Ray's vocals) and Air Studios (the choir) in early 2009. When the album was launched that summer, we performed 'Waterloo Sunset' on a beautiful evening next to Waterloo Bridge on the River Thames. In November, we toured the album to the West and East Coast in the US and appeared on the *Late Show With David Letterman*, using New York's Dessoff Choirs. One lovely memory was of a totally relaxed Ray and me swimming in the David Hockney pool at Los Angeles's Roosevelt Hotel. Many UK concerts followed, plus another US tour in 2011.

One aspect of Ray Davies that many may not know is that he is very interested in and knowledgeable about classical music, and he has followed my career as a conductor on top of the work we have done together. A very special memory was in Denmark in 2010 when we were travelling in a minibus and he – out of the blue – asked me if I could show him how to conduct the opening of Beethoven's 'Fifth Symphony' and also explain how that opening rhythm worked! Ray is exceptionally intelligent and has a head full of facts, details and memories – great to have on my pub quiz team, as once happened.

In 2011, our most important collaboration happened at London's Royal Festival Hall when Ray curated the annual Meltdown Festival. Along with Ray and his band, there was the 90-strong Crouch End Festival Chorus and the 80-piece London Philharmonic Orchestra. Along with the usual great Ray Davies hits, we performed a suite based on *The Kinks Are The Village Green Preservation Society* album from 1968. Another highlight was a similar concert in London's Hyde Park, where, this time, we were joined by the BBC Concert Orchestra for the Proms in the Park in 2017. This was the last time we performed with Ray, though we do keep in touch, often over a mushroom omelette and fries!

What is Ray like to work with? I simply loved working with him, and he, quite rightly, could be very exacting at times. Nothing was ever personal – he simply wanted everything to be the best it could be. My singers in the Crouch End Festival Chorus hold him in great affection and were thrilled when he agreed to become a patron of the choir. As a conductor, I have been lucky to work with many extraordinary musicians over many years – but for me, Ray is at the very top, partly because of his extraordinary abilities as a musician and songwriter but also because he offered me his friendship, which was and still is a treasure beyond words.

Temple co-founded the Crouch End Festival Chorus in 1984 and has served as its music director since its inception. In addition to the classical repertoire, the choir has collaborated with Oasis and Noel Gallagher as well as recording soundtracks for *Doctor Who*, *Good Omens*, *Prince Caspian*, and *Rocketman*.

1999
Around The Dial With … Carey Fleiner

In 1999, I wove a guitar strap for Dave, which I was able to give him after one of his shows. I'd been a weaver for a few years (and doing handwork for many more), so it struck me as an unusual yet practical gift.

I'd struck up an informal correspondence with Dave through his website's message board – he was keen to interact with fans, and he'd pop in and out with reflective thoughts and funny observations. Occasionally, we'd exchange emails that were quite fun – usually about cats and Monty Python rather than music. I attended many of Dave's solo shows when he toured the East Coast in 1999, and he and his entourage were very kind and generous; I was allowed to take photographs, for example, throughout the shows. This was in the days of film, and using a modest Nikon SLR, I accumulated probably about 900 or so photos of him, his band and the stage shows over the course of a few years.

The guitar strap was a way to repay him and the band for their kindness and for the times I was put on the guest list or otherwise gifted with wonderful experiences, such as attending soundchecks in the afternoons on a show date. On this occasion, it was in return for signing my Flying V guitar. The strap was made on my big 45-inch four-harness jack loom – these days, I would probably simplify my life and weave it on a tablet loom more fit for purpose, but it came out well. I used rug-weight cotton (again, these days, I'd use linen, which is sturdier and can bear the weight of a heavier guitar) in black and white, and I wove it into an old four-shaft pattern called Gothic Cross (from Marguerite Porter Davison's book, for any weavers out there familiar with it). I made it much longer than needed to give myself leeway; I've been playing guitar myself since I was a teen, so I know how long is comfortable and where to allow for take-up and adjustments. I still have the excess bits here with me, kept among my things when I moved permanently to England.

It was somewhat hectic getting the strap to Dave, as the original plan had been to attend shows as he and his entourage travelled up the US East Coast. We'd joined the tour when the band played in Atlanta, but there wasn't much of a chance to talk and visit until after the next show in Carrboro, North

Carolina, at the Cat's Cradle. We were invited backstage so Dave could sign my guitar and everyone could catch up and chat. Both he and his band (David Nolte, Dave Jenkins and Jim Laspesa) were tired but friendly – lots of silly bants back and forth by all. Dave D. was absolutely chuffed to receive the guitar strap, especially after he learned it was handmade.

We meant to attend the next night's show in Springfield, Virginia, but life got in the way. My transportation was fine for those first couple of shows, but the driver refused to continue after that, so I missed Springfield – friends contacted Dave and told him that I was trying to get to the third show. One of the band members said Dave had the strap wrapped around his microphone stand the night that I missed, but I've never seen a good photo to be sure.

We picked up the tour again in Atlantic City and then up the coast for a few more dates. It was lovely to see the band and visit with them before and after shows and a couple of times during soundchecks. Dave did use the strap for most of that tour and for later dates with his black Ovation – since it was a hollow body, it was lighter in weight and the strap could hold it. The Ovation was, sadly, destroyed by baggage handlers on a later tour, and the smashed guitar was sold to a collector. I don't know what happened to the strap, but I do have the photos, an unpublished but detailed tour diary that I wrote about this tour and several others and the other half of the strap itself.

Fleiner, a senior lecturer in classical and early medieval history at the University of Winchester, wrote the book *The Kinks: A Thoroughly English Phenomenon* (Rowman & Littlefield Publishers). She lives in Hampshire, UK.

Gerrit van den Berg – Badhoevedorp, The Netherlands

After a long time, I returned to where I grew up in Deventer, Holland. I once again stood in front of my parents' house and thought back to my real introduction to The Kinks' world. A then-friend lent me an LP and said, 'Play this, Gerrit – I think you're going to like it.' I put it on our record player, and after some crackling, I heard *The Kinks Kontroversy* album for the very first time. I was all alone, and it happened in our front room in Deventer. I awakened to a new musical world, 17 years young. I had heard 'You Really Got Me', 'All Day And All Of The Night' and 'Tired Of Waiting' before on my transistor radio and loved them. They had already made a big impression on me, and those were also Kinks songs! I listened, but now with special attention to the two albums that preceded *The Kink Kontroversy*. I was, as I can say in retrospect, hooked for life!

Many happy Kinks years later, I read Ray Davies' book, *X-Ray*. The parts of his story that stuck with me were those that took place in his family's front room growing up. In *Kink*, Dave also describes his experiences in this special room as a major influence in his young life. Many of their songs sprung from there. I wanted to visit that place, so in 1999, I finally travelled alone to North London and stood in front of 6 Denmark Terrace. I was impressed by the compact space where the magic of The Kinks blossomed. This space also 'housed' so many characters described by both brothers at the time. As I observed it all intently, a thought arose in me to turn it into a pencil drawing or watercolour painting instead of just a photograph.

Not once did I feel too curious – an intruder or, worse, a voyeur, a feeling I feared because this was someone else's life. No, Ray's story moved me with phrases like, 'It was like I felt closer to religion when I rehearsed with Dave in the front room.' The fragile smallness of the mysterious front room made a friendly, innocent, but also lone impression of a silent witness, strange but also familiar.

In 2003, working on a miniature, my thoughts went back to my trip to Fortis Green. It dawned on me: 'This might be the best way to make 6 Denmark Terrace – as a replica miniature for myself.' In April 2006, after his concert in Groningen, I showed Ray a photo of my completed miniature of his parents' house. I asked if he wanted it for himself, and he did. At Ray's next concert in Utrecht, I gave the 6 Denmark Terrace miniature to him.

The finest moment of giving Dave another miniature of his birthplace came at his last show of 2015 at London's Islington Assembly Hall. The fans – and Dave – got the biggest surprise when Ray appeared on stage. In the exciting atmosphere that followed, both brothers closed the show with the 1964 song that started it all: 'You Really Got Me'. All Kinks fans were overwhelmed, but a miracle happened for me and the lucky ones present. After all, the brothers had not appeared on stage together since 1996! To Dave's miniature, I added the legendary 'Green Amp' that had inspired the 'You Really Got Me' riff. Anyone who understands my admiration for this wonderful band will realise how happy I was to give Dave my miniature of 6 Denmark Terrace right after this historic reunion.

I think back to that first moment of my Kinks journey in our front room in Deventer. If I could, I would relive that overwhelming first impression of my first real Kinks encounter one more time. If only I could glimpse that part of my childhood, like taking a seat in a H.G. Wells time machine and being told: 'Let me take you on a little trip …'

'Play this, Gerrit – I think you're going to like it'. My old friend surely would be surprised!

Sean Higgins – Mount Laurel, New Jersey, US

In 1999, I found myself driving home, feeling depressed after losing my job. As I turned on radio station WMMR in Philadelphia, Pierre Robert, a longtime DJ and Kinks enthusiast, was introducing the next song. Pierre was one of the reasons I became a Kinks fan, and he always lamented how they never achieved the same level of fame as their British Invasion contemporaries like The Who, The Rolling Stones and The Beatles.

On this occasion, he was introducing 'Misfits' and went on a long monologue about how Ray Davies' words always managed to give solace during the most difficult of times. It felt like he was playing the song directly for me, and it seemed like Ray was giving me hope. Between the heartfelt introduction and the song itself, I felt a healing that reassured me that everything would be okay. When I got home, I promptly sent Pierre an email to the station to express my gratitude and share what the song meant to me.

    A few years later, an article in *Philadelphia* magazine featured a story on Pierre. In this article, he discussed his relationship with his fans and shared excerpts of some of the most meaningful fan letters he had received over the years. To my amazement, my letter was included. It's a memory I'll cherish forever.

The 2000s

As Ray Davies continued to tour with his stage show *The Storyteller* (through 2001), he reportedly also sought a record deal for solo albums of original material. Three shows in August 2000 at the 280-seat Jane Street Theatre in New York City, backed by indie-rock darlings Yo La Tengo, allowed him to showcase those new songs to label bosses in a venue full of supportive fans. In 2002, Ray began touring with a full band, with an opening acoustic set featuring him and guitarist Bill Shanley (who replaced Pete Mathison). Although he sometimes still read from *X-Ray* or told stories, it was more of a concert of independent songs. In addition to concerts around the US (and occasionally Canada) in the 2000s, Dave Davies toured Germany, Austria and the UK in 2002. That same year, *Bug* became his first fully produced solo album in nearly 20 years.

In late December 2003, Ray was named a Commander of the Order of the British Empire for his services to music – but less than a week later, a thief shot him in the leg after snatching his companion's purse in New Orleans' French Quarter (where Ray had been living). His injuries were worse than reported at the time, but he collected his CBE from Queen Elizabeth II in mid-March 2004. Dave had his own health setback in June 2004 when he suffered a stroke while leaving the BBC's Broadcasting House in London after an interview. After two months in hospital, he spent many months in physical rehabilitation, learning to walk, talk and play guitar again.

In 2005, The Kinks were inducted into the UK Music Hall of Fame. The event marked the last time that the four original members – Ray, Dave, Mick Avory and Pete Quaife – were together onstage.

Ray's long-gestating solo album, *Other People's Lives*, was released on V2 Records in early 2006, featuring several songs played at the Jane Street Theatre six years earlier. It reached the top 40 on the UK Albums Chart and number 122 on the *Billboard* 200. In late 2007, *Working Man's Café* (helmed by Ray and country/Americana producer Ray Kennedy) included several songs inspired by his time in New Orleans and the aftermath of the shooting.

That same year, Dave also released *Fractured Mindz*, a studio album reflecting on his stroke recovery, spirituality and concerns about society circa the mid-2000s. The songs range from hard rock and blues to trippy and experimental.

After working with Crouch End Festival Chorus conductor David Temple on several previous projects, Ray recruited the choir for the BBC's Electric Proms in 2007. Featured were choral arrangements for the Kinks classics 'Dedicated Follower Of Fashion', 'Waterloo Sunset' and 'Shangri-La'. An album, *The Kinks Choral Collection*, followed in 2009.

In 2008, the musical *Come Dancing* ran for six weeks at the Theatre Royal Stratford East. The story (like the song) was based on the Davies sisters' experiences at music halls and clubs in the 1950s. The music included three Kinks hits as well as new songs by Ray, who starred in the show as the narrator. A revival in 2010 was cancelled; a concert version with Ray and cast members had three performances at the Theatre Royal Stratford East in 2012.

Rumours of a Kinks reunion appeared periodically in the press.

Albums by The Kinks: *BBC Sessions: 1964–1977* (2001)
Albums by Ray Davies: *Other People's Lives* (2006), *Working Man's Café* (2007), *The Kinks Choral Collection* (2009)
Albums by Dave Davies: *Rock Bottom – Live At The Bottom Line* (2000), *Fragile* (2001), *Bug* (2002), *Transformation – Live At The Alex Theatre* (2003), *Rainy Day In June* (2004), *Fractured Mindz* (2007)

2000
Evan Spellman – Kirkland, Washington, US

I was eight years old in August 2000 when I made the flight from Colorado to Massachusetts with my mother to see Dave Davies at the Sit 'n' Bull Pub. My mom, who has had her photographs of The Kinks on some of their album covers and in books about them, played the band's music often as I grew up. The Kinks, outside of The Beatles, were the only band whose lyrics I could recite and whose looks and style I could recall – I would proudly wear shirts with their logo to elementary school.

Bringing a little kid into a rock club around a bunch of crazy New Englanders is probably prohibited for good reason, but my mother convinced the very nice owner of the club (also a big Kinks fan) to let me see the show, even though it was 21-plus. So, Gameboy in hand, I jumped into the car and off we drove from our family friend Doug's house to the club. As soon as we parked, I spotted the marquee with Dave's name on it. The doors opened, and we found a table close to the stage where I played Pokémon while we waited.

It seemed like a long time to wait in the cramped, dark bar, but I kept busy with my peanut butter and jelly sandwich, Gameboy and my mom's old Kinks friends to talk to. Finally, everyone was yelling, 'Dave! Dave! Dave!', as the band came on to grab their instruments, and then the man himself came up to the mic. 'Hello!' he shouted, and the entire place erupted.

I had never experienced anything like this – the energy, the commotion, the noise. It was shocking but in the best way possible. 'That's Dave!' I shouted at the top of my lungs as if anyone could hear me. That was the guy I had seen on albums, in my mom's old photos and on VHS recordings of television appearances, and I couldn't believe he was real. The Kinks and Dave seemed like entities that existed only in song.

The band started playing, and everyone around me sang the lyrics word by word with Dave. For the first few songs, I mashed my head between people in excitement and frustration, trying to get the right angle to see through arms, waists, legs and heads. My mom's friend Jason caught sight of me, picked me up and put me on his shoulders just as 'Lola' started so I could get a better view. This was amazing – the best experience of my life.

Thank You For The Days

It must have been around 1 am when the band finished playing. It was way past my bedtime, but I was wired. I had just danced and sung while listening to my favourite songs with a bunch of strangers in the dead of night, and I was grinning from ear to ear. We stuck around for a bit and waited for people to leave the club. I had no idea why we were doing this, so I just figured it was something that my mom and her friends always did.

After a while, someone came up to our little group and said, 'Hey, you guys can go back now.' Go where? Was she telling us to go home? I followed my mom as we walked down some stairs into a room and ... whoa, there was Dave Davies! 'Marianne, Doug!' he said as we walked in, and he gave my mom a hug and a kiss on the cheek. I stood speechless. Then he looked at me and said, 'Someone get this guy a beer – he must have just turned 21!' and everyone laughed. My first instinct was: 'Uh oh, am I in trouble?' I looked at my mom, and she was laughing, and then Dave came over and shook me by the shoulders and asked how I liked the show. 'Amazing!' was all I could muster. 'It was great to see you out there!' he responded and ruffled my hair before turning his attention to my mom and her friends and others as my mom directed me toward the food tables.

The other members of Dave's band saw me mowing through the food and laughed. They all asked if I liked the show and how old I was. Everyone was so friendly, and I felt strangely at home among all these musicians and older guys, but I was still eight years old and in front of me was a plate full of brownies calling my name. I sat down next to Jason and talked about the show with him, my favourite songs, and how much I knew about The Kinks, trying to impress him by knowing the names of the songs and the country the band was from.

Eventually, everyone was ready to go; the band's stuff was all packed up. My mom and her friends had talked with Dave for a while and she said it was about time that I got to bed. 'No, Mom, I'm not even sleepy!' I exclaimed, trying not to seem lame in front of the band, but no matter how cool I was hangin' out backstage after the show, I was still governed by the iron fist of my mother, and we said our goodbyes. Dave told me to come to the next show and that I was a cool little guy before he shook my hand. I was ecstatic.

As soon as we got in the car, I asked my mom, 'Did you hear what Dave said? He said I was cool!' 'Yes, I heard', she said, smiling a Mom-smile at me. Sure enough, it couldn't have been five minutes before I was out cold and slept in the back of the car the whole way back to Doug's house.

René Dellemann – Nijmegen, The Netherlands

Strangers on this road we are on
we are not two, we are one ...

In 1970, I was an ordinary lad growing up in a small village somewhere in the middle of The Netherlands. I had just graduated from secondary school and was at a loss about what to do next. Even though I was only 17, I knew I wanted to go to university and live on my own. The world was at my feet, but what was I heading for? No idea.

I decided to start studying English, mainly because I wanted to know what exactly The Kinks – my favourite band since 1966 – were singing about. Cryptic lines like 'the trainer of insects lies crouched on his knees, frantically looking for runaway fleas' somehow fed my appetite for remarkable quotations or significant lines from books and songs.

I ended up as an English teacher at a grammar school in Nijmegen for over 40 years. The lyrics of pop songs were frequently part of the lessons. Many lessons on Bob Dylan, John Lennon, Randy Newman, Leonard Cohen and, above all, Ray Davies were incorporated into my literature curriculum. *Schoolboys In Disgrace* was a must in the fourth grade each year, and I even had my students write essays on the album. 'Yes Sir, No Sir' and 'Some Mother's Son' were discussed alongside the war poems by Wilfred Owen and Siegfried Sassoon, and when a girl in the class named Lola had her birthday, she and her classmates were treated to the song and the unravelling of its extraordinary story.

In 2000, the school appointed a new headmaster. The old one – with whom I had not got on well – was replaced by a young one. In July, just before the holidays started, he came to our school to meet us, the staff of teachers that he was going to work with after the summer break. In a newsletter before he arrived, he described himself as a music lover, The Beatles and The Kinks being his favourite bands. Of course, my heart had jumped reading this, as followers of The Kinks were rare in those days. They had not performed since 1996, and for most music lovers, they belonged to the past.

So when Ronald, the future headmaster, was in the staff room shaking hands with everybody and naturally forgetting the names of all these new people, I thought up a little plan to make him remember me and put him to the test at the same time. When he walked up to me and asked my name, I said I shared my initials with a man he admired. I did not even have to add that this particular guy was in a band he liked because he mentioned Ray Davies right away. I looked him in the eyes and said I wanted proof that he was really a dedicated follower. Ronald looked at me, wondering what I was going to ask him. It was a decisive moment in our lives – we both felt that.

I said, 'I am going to quote a line from a Kinks song, and I would like you to add the line that comes next. Is that okay with you?'

I still could see the little flicker in his eyes. It was not something he could have foreseen when wondering how his visit to his new school would go.

'Ready?' I asked him, and then prompted: 'Preserving the old ways from being abused'.

Ronald replied immediately – he didn't even have to think: 'Protecting the new ways for me and for you – what more can we do?'

Our friendship started that day. Since then, we have spent many fine hours listening to and talking about the oeuvre of Sir Ray, and both of us agree on the literary quality of his work. Together with another Kinks follower – the father of four pupils at my school (how I met and befriended him is another story) – we spent a weekend in London, going on a pilgrimage to Kinks territory. We had lunch at The Clissold Arms, and we stood in front of the little house on Denmark Terrace where the Davies family used to live. We also saw the *Sunny Afternoon* musical at the Harold Pinter Theatre.

Let's all raise a glass to the rock stars of the past, especially those who made it!

2001
Around The Dial With ... Mark English

I'd always been aware of The Kinks but first became a fan when The Jam covered 'David Watts' and The Pretenders released 'Stop Your Sobbing'. Being name-checked by two of the biggest UK acts in the late 1970s gave The Kinks a certain kudos. Backed by a TV campaign, a best-of compilation called *20 Golden Greats* came out in September 1978 and reached number 19 in the UK album charts. My brother's girlfriend had a copy and allowed me to tape it. During the 1980s, I continued to check out their back catalogue, with *Village Green Preservation Society* becoming a particular favourite.

In November 1993, I finally saw the band live. Only Ray and Dave Davies remained from the original lineup, but it was still The Kinks. They rocked out at The Ritz Theatre in Lincoln, England. I remember them being heavier than I imagined, but the songs, musicality and stagecraft were without question.

A few years later, I was asked if I fancied forming a Kinks tribute band. The Kinks had ceased touring, and there was no one else in the UK flying their flag. Naturally, I jumped at it. From 2001 to 2012, Kinked played all over England to enthusiastic audiences, and we loved spreading the Kinks gospel. A highlight was supporting Dave Dee, Dozy, Beaky, Mick and Titch. They were great guys and full of stories about the halcyon days of the 1960s, including the time they appeared at the *NME* Poll Winners Party in 1966 with The Beatles, The Rolling Stones and The Who. The Kinks had appeared the previous year.

Although the tribute band called it a day over a decade ago, it was a great thrill when my new band, The Gold Needles, were asked to contribute a track for the *Jem Records Celebrates Ray Davies* album. We recorded two tracks: 'Village Green Preservation Society' and the early Kinks single 'You Still Want Me'. We kept back the second track for our new album. Not only was 'VGPS' one of our best-loved tracks but we liked the Englishness of it, particularly the imagery, which we thought might be confusing for non-UK listeners. We had grown up with the likes of Desperate Dan, and Old Mother Riley was a music hall stalwart who died in the wings of the Tivoli Theatre, Hull (our home city).

We did toy with the idea of resurrecting the Kinks tribute band for a one-off gig to celebrate King Charles' coronation, but we never got any further than 'God Save The Kinked'. Maybe another day.

English and The Gold Needles are based in Kingston upon Hull, UK.

James Swartz – Baltimore, Maryland, US

The first time I saw Ray Davies live was on 26 September 2001. I was nine years old. It was two weeks after 9/11, and the concert was at the State Theatre in Arlington, Virginia. I remember passing the Pentagon draped with an American flag as my parents drove to the concert. I went to school near Washington, DC, and the tragic events of 9/11 made me realise that the real world wasn't as great a place as my school had tried to paint it.

At the concert, we sat next to a reporter, and he was amazed at how I knew all the words to the songs. For me, 'The Journey' started when I was around four years old. I was outside with my dad while he was cleaning his car, and he told me to come listen to a song, which happened to be 'Have A Cuppa Tea'. I was hooked.

The next year when I was in kindergarten, I snuck my dad's cassette of *Muswell Hillbillies* into my book bag and asked my teacher if we could listen to that instead of the nursery rhymes that they played for us. She did not play it. I discovered more gems like 'Do It Again', 'Nine To Five' and 'Autumn Almanac'.

The concert at the State Theatre sent my love of their music to a new level. The power of seeing Ray performing 'Waterloo Sunset' live stuck with me. It was the first Kinks live show that I'd seen. Now I'm 32 and have seen more than 100 shows collectively of Ray, Dave and The Kast Off Kinks.

As a younger fan, I've felt like a misfit, like I should have been born 50 years earlier. I have always been able to relate to and find comfort in the music of The Kinks. There seems to be a song for every situation you find yourself in. Just last year, I woke up to discover 'somebody stole my car'!

Wayne Carey – Birmingham, UK

Having been regularly listening to The Kinks since the age of 14, buying the *Well-Respected Kinks* album on Marble Arch in 1966 and attending numerous concerts over the years – The Kinks, Ray and Dave Davies solo shows and The Kast Off Kinks – I have quite a repertoire of stories.

On 24 October 2001, Dave performed at JB's club in Dudley, England, as part of a few UK dates that (or any) year. It was a Wednesday evening, and about 130 miles away, Arsenal FC played Real Mallorca in an important European Cup match. Dudley is in the heart of England in an area known as The Black Country because of the pollution it generated during the Industrial Revolution. The evening was damp and dismal. The location of JB's was not the most salubrious, and the exterior lighting was the sort favoured by muggers and substance abusers. Praying my car would still be there post-concert, I hurriedly scuttled to the entrance and went in. It was just before 7:30 pm.

The next two hours were like something from Franz Kafka. The audience was frighteningly small. I'm not big on eye contact, but it was unavoidable as we huddled close to the bar as much as for warmth as for alcohol. One woman brought a toddler and her shopping in a buggy and parked it at the bar – which, I have to say, was a first for me at a gig.

The roadie/sound guy, a lovely American chap, struck up a conversation with me, and I learned an awful lot about his time with Dave and the band. Every once in a while, he'd come over and say, 'Dave will be out soon' or 'shortly' or some such. Each time, I politely said, 'No, he won't.' This went on until 9:10, when instead of saying 'no', I said, 'You could be right.' Within 20 minutes or so, Dave and the band joined us. How did I know? Because the Arsenal match was finishing up, and Dave could stop watching – or more likely listening to – the game to come out and play. He was on fire that night. It was a mighty concert, and he had an absolute ball. I later learned Arsenal won 3-1.

There may have been as few as 31 of us (including the toddler) at JB's that night, but I wouldn't have missed it for the world. Best of all, my car was still there with all its wheels as I floated back to it afterwards and listened to Dave's CDs all the way home.

Geri Tauber – Riverside, Illinois, US

It was 2001, just a few short weeks after 9/11. We had planned to visit London with our two sons and a nephew, and we decided to go ahead with the trip. Our plane from Chicago was nearly empty.

After the usual sightseeing – and threats to the boys that they would visit Kensington Place to see the exhibit of Princess Diana's clothes if they didn't behave – my husband Rick and I took them on a wee 'rock 'n' roll tour' of north London. First was the obligatory visit to Abbey Road. Next, back on the Tube to East Finchley and a walk to Denmark Terrace. We were hungry, so we popped into The Clissold Arms for lunch. Our youngest, nine years old at the time, was feeling the effects of jetlag and was, well, grumpy. He refused to order anything to eat. Our very patient server crouched down to eye level and asked, 'How are you feeling?' He replied, 'I miss my dogs.' To which she asked, 'What are their names?'

'Hercules and Lola', he said.

'I'll bet your parents are Kinks fans', she exclaimed.

Busted! We confessed that, indeed, we were dyed-in-the-wool Misfits.

'I want you to meet somebody', she said, moving swiftly away from our table. Minutes later, she returned with a smiling woman in tow.

'This is Olga!' she proclaimed. Olga smiled, pulled up a chair, and asked, 'Are you here for the castoffs?'

Hmmm. The what? What are castoffs?

Olga explained: The Kast Off Kinks are former members of the band who would be playing in two days' time at the Archway Tavern. You know, the pub featured on the cover of *Muswell Hillbillies*. 'But it's sold out', she added with sadness. 'Tell me where you are staying, and I'll see what I can do.'

The next day, our hotel gave us a message. 'Meet me at the Archway. I have five tickets for you!' The first miracle of Olga! We showed up that Sunday with three rather reluctant boys (ages 17, 16 and nine). Olga greeted us and, of course, sold us some raffle tickets!

Rick, who had been a Kinks fan since his teen years, was overwhelmed as he watched Mick Avory unload his kit from a van (by himself!) and set it up on the tiny stage. Mick reached out a hand to Rick and said, 'Good to meet you, mate!' I swear, I thought Rick was going to pass out.

The band trickled in, the music started and it was The Kinks! (Except the Davies brothers, of course.) Ray's ex-wife, Rasa, contributed background vocals. I found myself in a cluster of fans up in front, singing 'Alcohol' at the top of my lungs. Meanwhile, the boys were sitting as far away from us as humanly possible, clearly embarrassed at the spectacle we were making of ourselves. They thought the music was okay but declared it was 'fossil rock.' What did they know?

Fast-forward two years, and we were in Paris with the boys and Rick's dad. The Kast Off Kinks were playing at the Boston Arms, and Rick and I left the kids in the loving care of their grandfather while we took the train to London for the damn day and enjoyed our second KOKs performance. We made it back to Paris by midnight. All for the love of The Kinks.

We've been back many times for the Kinks Konvention weekend, as well as a couple of Ray's solo shows, and we count our Kinks friends among our dearest. Especially Olga.

Rob Kopp – Alphen aan den Rijn, The Netherlands

From 19-24 November 2001, I attended Ray Davies' songwriting course in Totleigh Barton in Cornwall, UK. There were 15 other students, including fellow Kinks fans Laurie Lyons and Julia Reinhart, and also Gerry, an opera singer who won the course and hadn't the slightest idea who Ray Davies was. I was the first student who didn't have English as his native language, but I was the only one who daily made an English breakfast!

Every day, you had to write two songs in your own room (I slept in Pigsty number two with just a bed, a table and a chair). Ray told you what a song should be about. In two or three hours, you just *had* to come up with something. Maybe you weren't completely satisfied, but at least the body of a song was there! We performed the results in central meetings from 11 am to 1 pm and 5-7 pm in 'The Barn'.

In daily one-on-one conversations with Ray, he told you how to improve your songs. The songs were the only thing that mattered in those talks. I didn't mention The Kinks once and didn't tell him about my book *Down All The Days*! (I finished the first edition on the day before The Kinks' concert at de Beurs van Berlage in Amsterdam on 1 July 1993. The only way I could think to get a copy into Ray's hands was by throwing it on the stage at the end of the gig!)

On Tuesday, just before dinner, Ray split us (the 16 students) into four groups of four people each. He said it was the first time he had tried this. At

5 pm on Wednesday, each group had to perform at least two songs. Ray gave our band the name Ben and His Big Brothers. Ben was 18 and by far the youngest student. We jammed and rehearsed all Tuesday evening, but when I went to bed, we still didn't have words or a melody, so I thought this would lead to nothing.

However, on Wednesday morning, everything we did the previous evening simply fell together. It was funny to see how Ben was writing the lyrics. He was just thinking in images. The words didn't rhyme at all, but his voice was so beautiful (a bit like Nick Drake) that it didn't matter. For me, 'Shooting Star' by Big Ben and His Brothers (we changed the band name a little) was the best song of the week.

On Wednesday, we were told we had to write a song about an incident in our lives. I decided to write about the hardest part of my divorce the year before – that I didn't see my two children on a daily basis. The working title was 'We're Okay', but Ray changed it to 'Miss The Kids'. Another suggestion he made: I had used the names of my children, Sebastian and Ingeborg, but Ray said that was far too personal (so what about Lola, Ray?). He told me I would reach a much bigger audience with 'your son' and 'your daughter' instead of those names, and I surely did!

After the course, I received messages from two Kinks fans in the same situation who said they had cried when they read the song's lyrics. Wow! And they hadn't even *heard* the song! Writing it was far more emotional than performing it. Maybe it was also a kind of therapy, but I was very satisfied with the result. More than ten years later, Brazilian Kinks fan Ayrton Mugniani wanted to cover the song, so I made a demo for him.

On Thursday night, we watched the film *American Beauty*. We had to turn that into a musical with 32 songs and perform it on Friday evening! What? But Ray said: 'You're already used to writing two songs every day, so what's the problem?' Karl and I played the gay couple, Jim and Jim. Here's our song, which we performed while nodding to each other:

We're partners for good, he's Jim, I am Jim
In case you haven't understood, he's Jim, I am Jim
An American beauty can be a lovely chick,
but an American beauty can also have a dick

A good example of Dutch humour, Ray said. Long live the late, great Annie M.G. Schmidt, the best musical songwriter The Netherlands ever had.
The musical *American Beauty* was simply fantastic. It's amazing what 16 people can achieve in one day. That songwriting course surely was one of the highlights of my life.

Hear the demo for 'Miss The Kids' at youtube.com/watch?v=pLeA1V_dsUs, with a short introduction at youtube.com/watch?v=156byshBX2o. Download

Down All The Days, a comprehensive guide to The Kinks, at *kindakinks.net/books/book-kopp.html*.

2004
Iñaki García – Barcelona, Spain

When I woke up in the ICU, I didn't know what day it was. We had travelled to Pamplona for the last weekend of June, and I became really sick. On Sunday (27 June), I was taken to hospital and that was the last thing I remembered. 'Is *The Village Green Preservation Society* already out?' It was one of the first things I asked, and it came as a surprise to my parents. That was quite a complicated title for a 16-year-old Spaniard to say, so they seemed relieved. It was proof that there was no significant brain damage. The deluxe edition of the *Village Green* album, the first to get such treatment, was out on 28 June, and I had been excited about it for months. At that time, The Beatles were my favourite band, but as I was getting more into The Kinks, they were a close second place. 'Yes, it's already Wednesday.' This was long before COVID, but my parents were dressed in protective equipment and masks, and there were almost tears of joy in their eyes as I spoke. I had been unconscious for three days and almost died. It turned out I had meningitis. In that same week, Dave Davies had his stroke – also a brain disease, something of a strange connection.

I spent three weeks in hospital, and to encourage my recovery, my parents promised that when I got better, we'd go to Liverpool, which was one of my dreams since I'd become a Beatles fan six years before. At last, I'd see the Cavern Club, Strawberry Fields and all the Beatles-related places. A few weeks later, when I was finally home, we started looking at flights for the first week of September. My father had the idea: 'Why don't you see if there are any cool concerts on those days in Liverpool?' I looked, and there was nothing of interest. But just a couple of weeks later, on 24 September, Ray would play there at the Philharmonic Hall. It was a Friday – a local holiday in Barcelona – and tickets were still available. It was perfect.

The concert was a blast. After everything I had been through, the joy of being in England for the first time and seeing Ray live, also for the first time, playing such an amazing show was indescribable. Before the concert, my father asked me: 'He won't play 'Death Of A Clown', will he?' It was one of his favourites. 'Nah, it's a Dave song – he never plays it live.' So, of course, the highlight of the show for us was when, on the second encore, Ray surprised the audience by singing 'Death Of A Clown', 'dedicated to my baby brother.' It was one of the very, very few times he played it. I know it wasn't true, but somehow, I felt he was also dedicating it to me.

I had brought the *Storyteller* CD with me, and I told one of the guys working at the Philharmonic that we came from Spain and asked if there would be any chance of Ray signing it. With great kindness, he asked me to give it to him, and he disappeared. A few minutes later, he came back with the CD signed by

Ray. I had never had an autograph or any real contact with one of my heroes before, so I was thrilled. He told us to go to the back door in a few minutes 'just in case.' When we got there, there were around 20 people waiting outside.

Soon after, a woman came out of the door and said something that my knowledge of the English language at that time didn't allow me to understand. But then people started to queue, so we did as well. They entered the building in groups of two or three people and stayed there for a short time before coming back with smiles on their faces. When I got closer, I saw the man through a window. Yes, it was Ray! My turn finally came, and we got in. He was incredibly kind, and I had a picture taken with him. At the time, it was the absolute highlight of my life, and to this day, it probably still is.

The whole weekend was great. We got to do the Beatles tour, see both cathedrals, enjoy a drink at the Cavern and have a really good time, but the best of all was seeing Ray live and meeting him. It was funny that, of all places, it was in Liverpool where The Kinks surpassed The Beatles and became my favourite band.

García is the co-author (with Manuel Recio) of *Atardecer En Waterloo*, a Spanish-language biography of The Kinks with a foreword from Dave Davies, and *Antología De La British Invasion* (with Álvaro Ortega), a history of 1960s British music.

2005
Lloyd Jansen – La Plata, Maryland, US
Rob Peirson – Irvine, California, US

Lloyd says: In the fall of 1979, when I was a senior at Apple Valley High School in the California High Desert, a friend named Tom Coleman, who was several years older, happened to be playing The Kinks' *Schoolboys In Disgrace* album when I visited him. It was a revelation for me. I had *Everybody's In Show-Biz* on eight-track, but in retrospect, that is not the album to be introduced to The Kinks. Listening to *Schoolboys* opened a whole new world. Soon after, I bought my own copy of the album, along with *Low Budget*, which was the current album at the time, and *Sleepwalker*. Discovering The Kinks was the most exciting thing since re-discovering The Beatles a few years before. I embarked on an obsession of finding everything I could by The Kinks.

Rob says: Back in the late 1970s, while living in Apple Valley, Calif., I was basically a radio music listener. In fact, the only song by The Kinks I knew was 'You Really Got Me', which had been covered by Van Halen. One day, Lloyd asked me if I wanted to go see The Kinks in concert, and I said that would be great – but could he make me a cassette mix tape so I could familiarise myself with some of their songs to better enjoy the show? I must have played that tape over a hundred times. Many of the songs I'd heard on the radio but had not realised they were The Kinks, and the ones I didn't know I thought were great. It was that mix tape and my first Kinks concert on 10 October 1980 at the Forum in Inglewood, Calif., in support of their live album *One For The Road,* that really began my Kinks konnection.

Lloyd and Rob say: In the early 1980s, we viewed The Kinks as a contemporary group. We had a vague understanding that they had a history, but for us, they were our favourite current band. As we waited for the next new album, we found older albums and discovered the music from their early prime, gaining an appreciation for their English roots. Through the 1980s and 1990s, we saw many Kinks shows and solo Ray and Dave Davies shows. We even made little MTV-like videos lip-syncing to The Kinks.

In the early 2000s, Rob lived in Irvine, Calif., and Lloyd was in Stockton, Calif. We were talking on the phone, reminiscing on our journey with The Kinks, and the idea of making a pilgrimage to Kinks London and Muswell Hill was born. We began intense research into their roots and decided to make a documentary of our journey, calling it *Two For The Road.* We made the trip to London in 2005 and filmed as we followed the band's roots in Muswell Hill and their family home at 6 Denmark Terrace along Fortis Green Road, with The Clissold Arms across the street, where Ray and Dave Davies first performed. We saw the schools they attended, possibly 'in disgrace.' We visited locations with connections to Pete Quaife and Mick Avory, as well as other places significant to the band.

We walked around Kinks London to Carnaby Street, Tin Pan Alley and many village greens. We explored important venues where they performed, as well as filming locations for videos like 'Starstruck', 'Dead End Street', 'Do It Again', 'Don't Forget To Dance' and 'State Of Confusion'. Most interesting were places connected to their songs, like Waterloo Bridge, Lavender Hill, Willesden Green, Holloway Prison, the site of the local Palais, and the Archway Tavern.

The highlight of our visit was Konk Studios, where the records we first got into were recorded. We finished at the location of the last Kinks show in London on 3 April 1995, at the Grosvenor House. Back in the States, we revisited the site of one of our most memorable Kinks shows: Glen Helen Regional Park, the site of the 1982 US Festival.

Our last Kinks adventure was our trip to London to see three performances of the *Come Dancing* musical, where we got to meet Ray in person. The last 44 years (and counting) as Kinks fans have made for many lasting memories.

See Rob and Lloyd's *Two For The Road* film online: Act 1: Everybody's In Showbiz (*youtu.be/9eqRl7_dGY4*), Act 2: Big Black Smoke (*youtu.be/qdWo93nV5wY*), Act 3: Something Better Beginning (*youtu.be/ZESrxUAmLNU*).

2008
Around The Dial With ... Jesse Laz
I've spent my entire music career chasing those Kinks guitar tones. In particular, the tone that launched 1,000 bands: 'You Really Got Me'/'All Day

And All Of The Night'. Later, 'Village Green Preservation Society' became somewhat of a theme song for our group and a key DJ track in sets we did.

On our 2008 tour backing up Ray, there are many fun memories. He was a big fan of our drummer, Sam Bair, who was the most technically proficient and professional musician in our group. I have a memory of him chanting, 'Sam, Sam, Sam, Sam ...', which we all thought was cool. By that point, he was doing the *Storyteller* thing and was less interested in the garage/punk thing that we were so enamoured by. I felt a little like the annoying younger brother who 'didn't get it yet.' It's funny as I reflect on this at the age of 40 because now I do get it. I like a cup of tea and some peace and quiet, not a bunch of drunken loudmouths trying to keep me up past my bedtime!

We did keep him up past his bedtime, though, at least twice. One time was in Atlantic City – it was the first time I ever played craps. He staked me and taught me the rules. I made him his money back with interest and earned a little for myself as well! Don't think I've played since.

Another memory was sharing a bottle of red wine after one of the shows – it may have been the last one. I asked about navigating a younger brother relationship in a band (my younger brother was in Locksley with me at the time). 'It's hard', he said. 'Good luck.'

Laz is the lead vocalist and rhythm guitarist for Locksley, a power-pop band based in Madison, Wisconsin, US, that toured with Ray Davies in 2008.

Around The Dial With ... The Minks

The Minks are the world's preeminent and possibly only all-female Kinks tribute band. We had a memorable meetup with the man himself back when The Minks first formed, around 2008, when Ray Davies played a solo show at the legendary Warfield Theatre in San Francisco, which is also The Minks' home base. We trooped to the show in our finest glad rags and kinky boots, fully loaded with Minks merch to hand out. It was a magical night – to enjoy so many favourite tunes with a sold-out crowd of enthusiastic Kinks and Ray Davies fans.

Our wildest dreams of meeting Sir Ray were realised after the show. As Ray walked down the long line of adoring fans, our familiar yet slightly different band logo caught his eye, and he made a beeline for us. Not only was it the thrill of a lifetime for us, but apparently, it was a memorable moment for Ray as well! Almost ten years later, we were shocked to see a Minks shout-out in the UK newspaper *The Sunday Post* on 27 January 2017. When legendary radio and TV presenter Paul Coia asked Ray about unusual Kinks covers or tribute bands, he replied, 'There's a fabulous all-girl band called The Minks who do a Kinks tribute act. Wonderful! Their motto is: 'The Kinks, but much less ladylike."

We feel beyond fortunate to have had that experience and to share our love of The Kinks' incredible music with the best fans out there. We hope to see The Kinks fans reading this book at a Minks show soon!

The Minks are Jenny Edwards (lead vocals), Allison Bennett (guitar), Linda Palermo (keyboards), Christina Michelle (bass) and Geri Vahey (drums). Learn more at facebook.com/theminksband.

2009
John Williams – Ilfracombe, UK

I have two passions/hobbies: I am a Tottenham Hotspur (Spurs) fan. I started following Tottenham when I was eight in 1963. I have also been a Kinks fan since 1964. Nothing wrong with that, you might assume – avidly following a fantastic football club and a fantabulous rock group. It was only in the late 1960s that I learned that Ray and Dave are fanatical Arsenal fans. As I got older and started to go to Tottenham games, I became aware of the intense rivalry between the two clubs. If you are at a Spurs vs Arsenal game, the atmosphere is electric, and the animosity between two sets of fans is all too obvious. So there it is: Ray and Dave will always support Arsenal, whereas I will always support their enemy. Incidentally, John Dalton is also an Arsenal fan. This contradiction always has been in the back of my mind.

In 2009, Dave opened a fete in Lynmouth. He sang the first verse of 'Village Green Preservation Society' and a song with a local group that I think he called 'The Lynmouth Blues'. When I got to talk to him, my opening gambit must have frightened him to death. I said, 'I have been having therapy because of you.' Dave remained unperturbed and asked me why. I replied: 'I have three loves in my life. My wife and children, The Kinks and … Spurs!' Dave laughed, and we talked for over 30 minutes. He was so natural and amicable. Dave said he liked Spurs and admired our attacking style. Yes, he acknowledged the rivalry, but he had Spurs friends and saw it more like neighbourly rows. He reminisced about seeing Arsenal ex-players when he went to games. You could tell he was a great Arsenal fan and a great football follower.

The conversation gradually drifted to music, and Dave told me he was trying to finish songs from the 1970s. Other things we talked about included John Dalton singing 'Willesden Green', Andy Pyle and Dave's love of *Arthur*. I mentioned I was seeing Ray at Hampton Court the following week and, to my surprise, Dave wasn't aware of it.

Eventually, I had to let Dave go as I felt guilty monopolising his time. He signed a photo of himself as follows: 'To John Spurs from Dave Gooner.' (Gooner is the nickname for Arsenal fans). He also posed with my wife and me for a photo taken by his then-partner, Kate. We shook hands and hugged, and as I left, Dave said to me: 'Good luck to Spurs next season.' The perfect end to one of the best days of my life.

And Ray? In 2018, I attended the Vox Holloway interpretation of the *Village Green Preservation Society* album. I am surprised this event hasn't gone down in Kinks folklore – it was so wonderful. Afterwards, I emailed Harvey Brough (the organiser, arranger and conductor of the event) and he said they were hoping to do a recorded version one day. Sadly, like a lot of Kinks hopes, this hasn't come to fruition yet. Ray attended both events and narrated some bits.

At the end of the 2018 concert, I had a quick chat with Ray. I used the same approach and mentioned receiving therapy to try to overcome my contradictory love of The Kinks and Spurs. Ray responded just as positively as Dave. He commented on the then-current Spurs team, saying he liked their style. Again, like Dave, you knew he was a great football fan just by the way he talked about the game. As for the contradiction, he said, 'North London rules', and punched his fist in the air.

Like with Dave, I was overwhelmed with his friendliness and comments. He had no reason to react like that. Time was short, and we had a quick chat about 'Starstruck' not being included in the performance. Another great day.

They say to never meet your idols. But what about meeting them and chatting about something they supposedly dislike? I did, and it just confirms that The Kinks aren't just a great rock band but they are also just great people who don't forget their fans.

One last word: When drummer Bob Henrit released his autobiography, he said he was a Spurs fan! That must have made for some interesting banter with Ray and Dave, especially on match days.

The 2010s

Inspired by a collaboration with Big Star's Alex Chilton – which turned out to be his final recordings before his death in 2010 – Ray Davies assembled an all-star cast to revisit Kinks favourites for *See My Friends*. Also appearing on the album were Metallica, Bruce Springsteen, Jon Bon Jovi, Jackson Browne, Mumford & Sons, Paloma Faith, Black Francis, Billy Corgan of The Smashing Pumpkins, Spoon and Lucinda Williams. Released by Universal, it reached number 12 in the UK albums chart.

After being diagnosed with renal failure in 1998, founding Kinks bassist Pete Quaife died on 23 June 2010. Dave Davies remembered him as 'a true musician, a true artist and an immensely gifted man full of life and love who was never really given the credit he deserved for his contribution and involvement' with the band. During a performance at the Glastonbury Festival on 27 June, Ray Davies told the crowd, 'I wouldn't be here today if it wasn't for him', and he teared up as he sang 'Days'.

In 2011, Ray curated the London-based Meltdown Festival with performances by The Crazy World of Arthur Brown, The Legendary Pink Dots, Yo La Tengo, Nick Lowe, Madness and others, as well as a tribute to the 1960s television music programme *Ready, Steady, Go!* The final concert at the Royal Festival Hall featured Ray with the London Philharmonic Orchestra and the Crouch End Festival Chorus.

A summer 2012 tour of Ireland, the UK and the West Coast of North America included Ray's final US concert to date: 22 July at the House of Blues in San Diego, California, backed by guitarist Bill Shanley and American band The 88. They ended the tour at the Fuji Rock Festival in Japan. A couple of weeks later, on 12 August, Ray performed 'Waterloo Sunset' as part of the 2012 Summer Olympics closing ceremony in London.

For his mid-2013 album *I Will Be Me*, Dave Davies recruited punk, power-pop and country-rock collaborators, such as Anti-Flag, The Jigsaw Seen, Ty Segall and The Jayhawks, for a stylistically diverse set of new songs. Opening track 'Little Green Amp' recalled The Kinks' early days and echoed the riffs from 'You Really Got Me' and 'All Day And All Of The Night'.

In the fall of 2013, Ray released his memoir *Americana* (with slightly different subtitles for the UK and US editions), which explored his complicated relationship with the US, its music and its people. Among other stories, he discussed his time in New Orleans, how a mugger shot him there and his recovery. The book led to UK appearances with Shanley in 2014, featuring readings and short films of The Kinks on tour.

Sunny Afternoon, a jukebox musical with Kinks hits and deep cuts, opened in May 2014 at the Hampstead Theatre in Camden. The book, written by Joe Penhall, told the early years of the band's career, their rise to fame and the drama behind the scenes. The show transferred to the West End's Harold Pinter Theatre in October. It won four Olivier Awards in 2015, including Best New Musical and the Outstanding Achievement in Music award for Ray. After playing in the West End for two years, a UK tour followed in 2016.

As part of his tour supporting his 2014 album *Rippin' Up Time* and its live follow-up record, Dave returned to the UK in December 2015 for a concert at the Islington Assembly Hall in London. Near the end of the show, Ray surprised the audience by appearing onstage to sing 'You Really Got Me' with his brother – the first time they had performed together in public for almost 20 years.

Ray received a knighthood in the 2017 New Year's Honors List for services to the arts; Prince Charles knighted him at Buckingham Palace in March. Later that year, he released the *Americana* album, with *Our Country: Americana Act II* following in 2018. Backed by The Jayhawks, Ray revisited and expanded on the themes from the 2013 book with new tunes and a couple of reimagined older songs, as well as spoken-word monologues. Taken together, the albums sounded like a stage show similar to *The Storyteller*.

Ray last played live for the BBC Proms in the Park event on 9 September 2017.

Dave's 2018 album *Decade* compiled 13 solo tracks recorded at Konk Studios in the 1970s, a period when few of his contributions were included on Kinks albums. Critics compared the vibe to The Faces or The Pretty Things and speculated that some songs could have been hits for the band.

Dave performed his last concert to date on 21 April 2019 at City Winery in Chicago, Illinois.

Longtime Kinks bassist Jim Rodford died in 2018 at the age of 76 after a fall at home. Keyboard player Ian Gibbons died from cancer in 2019 at age 67.

In 2019, BBC Radio 4 aired a radio play to celebrate the 50th anniversary of the *Arthur* album. Written by Ray and playwright Paul Sirett, it merged some of the original ideas for the 1969 television play (which was never made) with details about The Kinks' early career.

Rumours of a Kinks reunion appeared periodically in the press.

Albums by Ray Davies: *See My Friends* (2010), *Americana* (2017), *Our Country: Americana Act II* (2018)
Albums by Dave Davies: *I Will Be Me* (2013), *Rippin' Up Time* (2014), *Rippin' Up New York City – Live At The Winery NYC* (2015), *Open Road* with Russ Davies (2017), *Decade* (2018)

2010
Steve Goldstein – Redondo Beach, California, US
'Hi, I'm Ray', he said, reaching out to shake my hand in a backstage corridor at The Grove in Anaheim. As if I need an introduction to this particular man, whose career as a legendary singer-songwriter and frontman of The Kinks I have followed obsessively for well over 35 years. I am shaking the hand that wrote such classic songs as 'Lola', 'You Really Got Me', 'Sunny Afternoon', 'Shangri-La', 'Waterloo Sunset' and the hauntingly gorgeous 'Celluloid Heroes'.

Only two days before, I impulsively bid online for this once-in-a-lifetime opportunity to shake this hand, attend this show and pose for a photograph with my idol, the composer of the soundtrack to my life. I never dreamed I would make the winning bid and be standing here with my wife two nights later, getting preferential treatment over the others who held backstage passes and waited patiently for us to have this meeting before they were allowed backstage themselves.

I am no stranger to Kinks shows, having attended well over 60 of them since 1975, as well as numerous solo shows by Ray Davies since the band broke up. In fact, it had been just five months since I saw him at the Orpheum Theater in Los Angeles touring his album *The Kinks Choral Collection*, on which he reimagines many of his classic songs with a full choir. And only a year before that, we saw him at the Wiltern supporting his second solo album, *Working Man's Café*.

But that night, with no new album to flog, Ray was free to relax, have some fun and play whatever old chestnut popped into his head. And indeed, he reached deep into the Kinks katalogue to pull out some rare gems, some never performed live before, such as 'Two Sisters', a '60s-era thinly veiled ode to the complicated relationship he shares with his younger brother, Kinks lead guitarist Dave Davies; 'Nothin' In This World Can Stop Me Worryin' 'Bout That Girl', written when Ray was 17 and featured prominently in the film *Rushmore*; and one of my favourite album cuts, 'Too Much On My Mind'.

Starting the show as he had for the past decade by walking out with an acoustic guitar and accompanied only by guitarist Bill Shanley, Davies kicked things off with the anthemic 'This Is Where I Belong', and I could not have felt more connected to the song as, indeed, there was nowhere else on Earth I would have rather been at that moment than in that seat with my wife listening to this man perform this song.

From there, he continued with a set that included 'I Need You', 'I'm Not Like Everybody Else', 'Apeman', '20th Century Man', 'A Well-Respected Man', 'Sunny Afternoon', a rocking 'Victoria', 'See My Friends', 'Where Have All The Good Times Gone?' (played in November with the full rock band treatment but presented here acoustically) and 'All Day And All Of The Night' (yes, played during the acoustic portion of the show). He also debuted 'Postcard From London', a song about breakups that he recorded with his own ex (and mother of his 27-year-old daughter), Chrissie Hynde of The Pretenders.

Then, Davies brought back the opening band, The 88, for the electric portion of the show, tearing through 'You Really Got Me', 'David Watts', a tight and powerful 'Celluloid Heroes', 'Low Budget' and the show-closing 'Lola'. There was no encore, even with the crowd in a frenzy, but selfishly, this was fine with me because it meant I was that much closer to the after-show meet-and-greet.

Indeed, following the concert, Jennifer and I were escorted backstage to meet Ray. We had contributed to a music charity for the seats and the chance to say hello, pose for a picture and get one autograph. Ray could not have been nicer. First off, he said he recognised us from the audience. Secondly, he suggested a second photo when he felt the first one might have been too dark. He was warm, friendly and a tad shy. He graciously answered my question about where exactly he had been staying in Hollywood in 1972 when he wrote 'Celluloid Heroes'.

I had to fight the emotion of the moment. He and the promoters thanked us profusely for our generosity in supporting the charity. Thanked *us*! I could not thank them enough for the privilege. I am so happy to see he was the class act I knew he would be. Imagine if my idol had turned out to be a jerk! But no, Ray Davies is as sweet and generous as he is talented and entertaining. I said it to him, and I repeat it here: 'Thank you for writing the soundtrack to my life.'

Anna Martonfi – The Hague, The Netherlands

I grew up in socialist/post-socialist Eastern Europe (Hungary) and am a huge Anglophile. I've been a fan of all things 1960s and British since I was around ten or 11, courtesy of an older brother with good taste. He first shared Beatles songs and Monty Python – for quite a long time, it was these two that occupied my fan brain. I knew The Kinks and some of their songs from the radio, but it wasn't until my mid-20s that I became a real fan. I thought I'd grown out of fangirling over a band, but apparently, I hadn't, and the period when I regularly went to Kinks events was one of the nicest times in my life.

A few different things happened roughly at the same time that seemed to point to The Kinks: I was finishing my studies (English literature and linguistics), and because I had to learn a lot about 20th-century British politics and culture, I read Andrew Marr's praise for The Kinks as a quintessentially British/English band. I also noted three songs by The Kinks on the soundtrack for the film *The Darjeeling Limited*. And then, during the Christmas holidays that year, I was at my Dutch in-laws' home and heard The Kinks on the countdown radio programme Top2000. After that holiday, I looked up everything I could at the library and on the internet.

I saw that Ray Davies was still performing, so I started daydreaming about going to see him. I hadn't been to a lot of gigs at that point – I'd seen Bob Dylan when he played in Budapest, and it was great that I could tick that box, and I'd been to some concerts at Sziget (the music festival in Budapest), but I'd never gone abroad for a concert. (I'd not gone abroad that much at that point, full stop.) Quite uncharacteristically of me, I booked a ticket to a 2010 concert in Cambridge and went to see him – yes, that changed everything. I expected a similar experience to the Dylan gig, like a tick-in-the-box, but this was something else (pun not intended). It was an amazing gig – the music was fantastic, and so was he with his energy and enthusiasm.

I plucked up my courage and planned to ask for an autograph after the show, but he must have left through another exit, so I ended up waiting with this eclectic, inclusive, open, lovely group of fans. I went home to Budapest, but I couldn't just leave it at that – I had to go back! So, again, completely uncharacteristically of me, I called in sick to work and booked tickets for the last two gigs of that tour (London and Liverpool). To this day, it's the single craziest thing I've ever done, and it was absolutely, completely worth it – I loved every minute!

When I got to London, I reconnected with some of the fans I'd met in Cambridge and met Mick Avory at the stage door of the Royal Albert Hall. The gig was just as amazing as the Cambridge one, though there was still no sign of Ray after the show. The day after the London show, we all made our separate ways to Liverpool, but problems with the railways meant everyone was delayed. I got to the venue around 4 pm, and apparently, I was the first one there. I had a chat with the supporting band, The 88, who were all sweet. I also had a chat with keyboardist Ian Gibbons, who was the first of Ray's band to arrive, and he was such a lovely man to talk to. Then I saw Ray coming our way. I'd brought with me a tiny bottle of this weird Hungarian booze (Unikum), so I asked him if I could give that to him. He gave me a hug and a kiss on the cheek, and our sunglasses sort of bashed together, but I thought it was such a sweet moment. I didn't ask for an autograph or a photo; I just asked if he was well, and he came across as a surprisingly normal guy, albeit a bit shy.

I went to shows with Ray and the Kast Off Kinks quite regularly for the next couple of years, and I still have that pair of sunglasses (I call them the Ray sunglasses), although they're a bit frayed now. Other than the sunglasses and the autographs and photos I've collected, the most important part of Kinks fandom for me has been the love and support of the other fans – without them, I wouldn't have gone to so many gigs and events. It's a peculiar sort of connection but a strong one, and I know my life has been richer since the online and occasional offline contact with these lovely people.

2011
Kasia Kaszkowiak – Tampa Bay, Florida, US
Hearing 'Waterloo Sunset' in early 2011 made me an instant Kinks fan. I am happy that it got the ball rolling, but a part of me is sad that I was late in discovering the greatness of The Kinks and the unmatched storytelling of Ray Davies. Being born in 1995, it was out of my control to explore this music sooner. Fortunately, this critical moment of hearing 'Waterloo Sunset' inspired me to cram all my Kinks studies into a short time, and I wanted to see a Ray Davies concert right away. It was perfect timing because Ray was set to play in Atlanta, Georgia, in November. In preparation, I read *X-Ray*, bought Kinks records and binge-watched documentaries and interviews. Ray was a person that I started to become more curious about and started to feel connected to. The detached individual that Ray wrote about in 'Waterloo Sunset' matched

how I saw myself. I've worked quite a bit to get out of my shell, but during my early years in school, I was just a quiet mouse. Seeing the connections, it became a dream to meet Ray one day.

On 1 November, I skipped a day of school and drove up from Tampa Bay, Florida, to see Ray at Center Stage Theatre in Atlanta. Not having prior knowledge of meeting musicians, my mom and I went early to the venue to ask around. The sound guy suggested that we wait at the stage door near 3 pm. The suggestion worked. Ray came for the soundcheck, and only a few fans were there to ask for autographs and photos. It was my big chance to talk to Ray, but I blankly stared at him and handed over my copy of *X-Ray* to sign. Words were not working out for me. To break the ice, my mom – after accidentally calling him Dave – told Ray that I was shy, and he replied, 'No, she's beautiful.' I felt instantly accepted. It was just a surreal moment. If that wasn't enough, I had a third-row seat at the show, and Ray acknowledged me with a thumbs-up.

If the story ended there, it would still be ideal, but it's just started. I was blown away by my interaction with Ray. This led me to book my first trip to London in April 2012 for my 17th birthday. There's a Ray Davies tune called 'London Song' with the line, 'But if you're ever up on Highgate Hill on a clear day, I'll be there'. I had the determination to test out that line's legitimacy. On my first day in London, my mom and I managed to get to the Highgate Underground station but got lost in a neighbourhood and had no luck with directions. The second day, we persevered. My mom, being intuitive, was certain that we would run into Ray, and you know moms are always right. As we were walking in Highgate, my mom said, 'We're walking here, but he's probably behind us on the other side of the street'. Sure enough, there Ray was! My mom recalls that I ran over to him in a split second while she was still computing what was happening. I remember running over to enthusiastically say hello to Ray. Although Ray was confused, he politely asked what I was doing here. I guess the American accent gave it away. I explained that it was my spring break, and I was exploring London. It was enough. Ray was extremely pleasant about the situation. I asked for an autograph on a photo I brought along, which was of us from our first meeting in Atlanta, and I remember Ray's level of attention when finding the right spot to sign. After a quick chat, Ray said he was off to Konk Studios. That Highgate meeting was a pivotal point and stuck with me. The next time I saw Ray for the 2012 West Coast tour, he joked if I lived in Portland or Highgate.

I'm fortunate to say I continued to know Ray over the years and became a habitual London visitor. I now have my own Oyster card! In recent years, I even had the opportunity to tour Konk Studios with my parents – something my 16-year-old self just dreamed of doing. Ray has been incredibly kind to me and helped me through my coming of age. I'm extremely grateful for everything.

Roel Bakker – Groningen, The Netherlands

In the early 1980s in the Netherlands, many new singer/songwriters and their bands performed songs in Dutch. Because musicians sought (and still seek) a wider audience, most songs were in English. Het Goede Doel (The Good Cause) with singer Henk Westbroek was my favourite. His lyrics always told a little story about his experiences.

Circumventing the 1990s ban on tobacco advertisements, Marlboro started the Marlboro Flashback Tours. Well-known artists played songs by their favourite musicians in small venues. In 1991, Westbroek – a huge Kinks fan – visited my town (Groningen) with Kinks songs. I recognised the songs as the ones I always liked but had forgotten. A leaflet at the venue advertised the Dutch Kinks fan meeting. There, I heard of the official fan club in the UK, which led me to visit the upper floor of the Archway Tavern (and later the Boston Arms) to hear the Kast Off Kinks and others. Soon, the internet became available for everybody at home, and I paid a daily visit to Dave Emlen's website, KindaKinks.net.

After 1996, The Kinks were not performing any longer, and the Davies brothers went solo. Ray came to Dutch theatres with his *Storyteller* tour and a few other concerts. Dave was based in the US but finally did a European tour and came to Berlin at the Jazz Keller Quasimodo in October 2001. Dave's energetic playing appealed to me, and I wanted to see and hear him again. The next opportunity came in June 2004, the Stadtwerke Open Air Festival in Potsdam, Germany. The sky cleared when Dave took the stage with his son Simon on drums, Derrick Anderson on bass and Jonathan Lea on guitar. The concert was recorded and later released as the live album *Rainy Day In June*.

This was the last gig I saw before Dave had a stroke that kept him out of the music scene for a few years. The announcement in 2011 about a Satsang at Dave's home in Devon, UK, was the first sign he was back. I called for details: a weekend of spiritual healing and yoga sessions, with each day ending in Dave's music room. It was expensive, but if I could find another person to go with me, the fee was bearable. A friend, a dedicated fan of The Who, was interested.

We took a plane to Bristol and a taxi to the Taunton railway station, then boarded a minibus to take the Satsangers to a secret location. That turned out to be a village near the Devon coast where hotel rooms had been reserved not far from Dave's premises. The next day (17 September 2011), the 25 Satsangers were introduced to Dave and got hugs!

After a long day of spiritual sessions by Rosina Mostardini and a round with the talking stick and meditation, we gathered in the music room. It was a relief to find that Dave could still make his Telecaster fill the room, although his voice was unsure. The band included Jonathan Lea on guitar, David Nolte on bass, Kristi Callan on backing vocals and drummer Frank Rawle on a cajon (there wasn't room for a drumkit). We enjoyed Kinks favourites along with Dave's songs and new material.

The participants exchanged names and suggested keeping in touch online. It was a life-changing experience as I learned to appreciate Facebook for allowing contact with other Kinks fans and family, as well as re-meeting friends from long ago. We went home on Monday, impressed by what a kind, sweet and emotional person Dave is.

In later years, Dave toured the US and came back to the UK only twice: at the Barbican (11 April 2014) and the Islington Assembly Hall (18 December 2015). The Islington show was the most remarkable because Ray came on stage for the 'You Really Got Me' finale! Of course, I was at both.

Shortly before COVID-19 put a hold on gigs, young female singer/songwriters Froukje and S10s became popular with songs in Dutch. It is impressive how they express their emotions in a poetic way about what is going on in the world and in their lives. For new generations, The Kinks are from the past, but music that tells a story will live forever.

Eva Anna Schiele – London, UK

I arrived at the party kind of late, compared to most fans – but I'm glad I did. As a child, I had the radio on all the time, so I recognised much of the music from the 1960s. I can't always name the artists, but the songs remain in my head. One evening in 2011, I was channel-hopping and came upon this interesting man talking about his life in a band. I didn't have a clue who he was, but I listened intently. Eventually, he mentioned The Kinks, and I was hooked. I had to know more, and it started my journey into Kinkdom. Since then, I have learned so much about the decade in which The Kinks started their musical career, and it has been an amazing awakening in many ways. It also was exciting to discover the enormous body of work and to read many of the books connected to The Kinks. The most significant discovery: although the band had stopped performing, their dedicated fans all over the world continued as if the band were still together. I was able to meet so many special people with one thing in common – a love for The Kinks. The music resonates with every fan. The songs often have very British themes, but all nationalities can identify with the intrinsic message that we are all human and we all experience the same problems. The Kinks fan is a special person who has a love for a melodic tune set to a lyric that defines a specific place in time. Ray has been able to write an account of events and feelings that he has captured and moulded into a few minutes of sound and storytelling like no other artist. Kinks fans gather, although we are scattered all over the world. Long may we all continue.

2013
Tom Rotnem – Atlanta, Georgia, US

One of the first times I saw The Kinks was in the early 1980s. I lived in Cleveland, Ohio, and grew up during the 'stadium' era. The concert was at the

Music Hall in downtown Cleveland, and when it was time for Dave to preview one (or more?) songs from his first solo album, *AFL1-3603*, he played 'Imagination's Real'. It was my first 'listen' to any of Dave's solo work. I instantly fell in love with that song!

In 2013, I bought tickets for the first three shows that Dave performed since he suffered a stroke. The venue was the City Winery in New York City. I went to the first show with my teenage son, and we sat in the second row right in front of Dave. It was a great show, and I stayed after to see if he'd come out and greet fans. He did, and I told him that I'd be seeing him the next night with my wife and asked if he could play 'Imaginations Real'. I told him that we had our DJ play the song at our wedding long ago. He told me to 'just call it out' and I assumed he'd play it. Well, the next night, I must have been very annoying to a lot of fans because I kept calling it out at that very small venue (maybe 300 people). Yet, he never played it! I guess it wasn't part of his setlist on the tour and he wasn't ready to play it. Oh well. I played it for us anyway on our way home as I pulled up the version from his *Rock Bottom* live album – an excellent version, to be sure.

2014
Around The Dial With ... Mark Doyle

In 2014, I was teaching a college class on 20th-century British history and was looking to bring some music in. The class met twice a week for 85 minutes at a time, which is an awfully long time to hold the interest of anyone, even when you're covering such sexy topics as coal mining, wartime rationing or the National Health Service. It's good to shift gears every 20 minutes or so, and one of the ways I did this was by playing some music either from or about the period we were studying.

The first part of the semester was easy. We listened to World War I trench songs, a little Motörhead, a little jazz from the BBC. Then we hit World War II, and, instead of playing something obvious like 'We'll Meet Again', I went searching for songs about the Blitz. That's how I found 'Mr. Churchill Says' from The Kinks' 1969 album *Arthur (Or, The Decline And Fall Of The British Empire)*. Now, I already knew and appreciated The Kinks. I even considered myself something of a fan, albeit a haphazard one: I grabbed at their songs as indiscriminately as a child grabbing at cake. And somehow, this album – not just the song, but the whole album – had eluded me.

I am a historian of British imperialism, so the album's title was what grabbed me first. Listening to the song, I was struck both by the historical accuracy of the lyrics (verbatim quotes from Winston Churchill and references to Lord Mountbatten, Lord Beaverbrook and the Spitfire fund) and by the fact that I couldn't work out whether it was celebrating or satirising the patriotic 'Blitz spirit' of the time. This, I later decided, was one of the things that I loved about The Kinks: You could listen to their songs a bunch of different ways, and each one would be valid.

So, I played 'Mr. Churchill Says' for my class, and I'm pleased to report that a few students – those who weren't absorbed in their phones or running off to the restroom – were seen to tap their feet. A head or two might have bobbed. I decided I would play them 'Shangri-La' when we got to the unit on postwar housing and suburbanisation. The next time I taught this class, I would play 'Yes Sir, No Sir' or maybe 'Some Mother's Son' during our unit on World War I. Hell, I thought, I'll begin the class with 'Victoria' and just go through the album track by track until we hit the 1960s, when we'll shift to David Bowie or something. Or maybe I could teach the whole class just using The Kinks. Weren't their songs a kind of sociological record of 20th-century Britain? The hopes and glories, yes, but also the failings and snobberies and disillusion and resilience?

I got a little carried away. Not only did I subject a whole generation of Tennessee college students to the glories of *Arthur* but I ended up writing a book about The Kinks – two books, in fact. The first one, which has mercifully never seen the light of day, was a novelisation of *Arthur*. That album was supposed to be the soundtrack to a television play, but the play never got made. Using the liner notes as a guide, I filled in what I thought might have been the story, almost certainly taking the characters in directions that nobody intended and inventing scenarios that were improbable. (I remember one scene where two characters get into a scuffle with a West Indian immigrant on the day of Queen Elizabeth's coronation.)

But that book led me to write another book about how Ray Davies' songwriting drew from and told the story of recent British history and culture. It functions a little like my classes, using Ray's songs to illuminate some of the changes that Britain (especially working-class Britain) went through during the 20th century. Although I have not been so gauche as to assign my own book to my classes, I have been informed by a few students that not only have they bought the book on their own initiative but that they enjoyed it, too. Whether it has turned them into Kinks fans is a separate question that I am not quite brave enough to ask, but one can hope.

Doyle is a professor of history at Middle Tennessee State University and the author of *The Kinks: Songs Of The Semi-Detached*. He lives in Nashville, Tennessee.

Ksenia Nemchinova – St. Petersburg, Russia (now Belgrade, Serbia)

I'd been aware of The Kinks musical *Sunny Afternoon* being developed since its first workshop in late 2012. However, having a bit of prejudice against musicals in general and jukebox musicals in particular, I wasn't sure how much I wanted to see it. Of course, I knew I'd do it one way or another, provided it materialised at all – so when Hampstead Theatre in London announced its run in spring 2014, I booked a ticket and started to wait. I had very low expectations, hoping that at least the arrangements of the songs would be good. Long story short, I booked my second – and third – visit during the interval.

Having attended various theatre productions in the UK, I could tell almost from the start that this show was special, not because I'd been a Kinks fan for ages, but perhaps even despite that. I'm very protective when it comes to their music and legacy, so I was relieved by what I saw. Yes, Hampstead is not a huge West End theatre, but that's what made that initial run unique – it allowed people to get closer to the story, revisit what they already knew or just learn something new.

It's by no means a documentary, but it's true to the story of the band – and then we have the music. I find it difficult to overestimate the craftsmanship involved in creating the arrangements of The Kinks' well-known songs. Being very theatrical, they create a perfect soundtrack to the story. I remember how astonishing it seemed that very few changes had been made to the lyrics to make the songs part of the story or the characters' dialogue. That's my main issue with jukebox musicals: You have the story, and you have the songs that exist as if by themselves. Here, they're integral to the plot, as if Sir Ray had been writing this musical his whole life.

Having seen the show at the Hampstead Theatre four times, including its closing night, I knew it was bound to transfer to the West End, so the announcement was not a surprise. I spent the next two years at the Harold Pinter Theatre, watching the show over 100 times, with both its original cast (most of them having transferred from the initial run) and the second cast. My friends and I had a lot of fun getting to know them, watching the understudies and their interpretations of the characters. Yes, I made some good friends going to see *Sunny Afternoon* – most of them have become very close because we had much more in common than our love for good theatre and good music.

In 2015, the show was up for five Olivier Awards, the most prestigious theatre award in the UK. We just had to be there – we couldn't miss it, even though they had some tough competition. It was my first – and only! – time walking the red carpet, since the Royal Opera House in London, where the ceremony was held that year, had only one entrance for the guests and the general audience. To our shock and delight, the show won four out of five awards, including Best New Musical, and even though it seemed like a dream, everyone I knew was over the moon. We were exhausted by the end of the evening from cheering and happy crying, but that is one of those days I'll remember all my life.

By the end of the show's two-year West End tenure, the UK and Ireland tour was announced. From August 2016 to May 2017, I travelled to some really nice and really obscure places in the UK, visited Dublin for the first time, made some new friends and generally had a great adventure. Now I also know which venues to avoid, like the plague, if I decide to follow any other tour in the future!

When it all came to an end, it was a bit sad, of course, but the three years I'd spent following *Sunny Afternoon* are among the most memorable ones of my life. I ended up seeing the show 179 times (and that's not even close to being the record!), 61 for each West End cast and 57 for the tour. I'd hoped to make the number equal for all three, but I had to cancel a couple of visits for various reasons. The producers did announce another tour for 2020-21, but the universe had other plans, so they pulled the plug and it's been quiet ever since. I don't know if I'll ever follow *Sunny Afternoon* as extensively as I did, but I'm looking forward to hearing what's next for the show.

Anders Johansson – Ornskoldsvik, Sweden

In May 2014, a friend and I travelled from northern Sweden to London to see the musical *Sunny Afternoon* at Hampstead Theatre, a small theatre in northern London. Just when the musical started, the theatre director came on the stage and announced that the man playing Ray had become ill and therefore the show had to be cancelled. We were booked into another event the day after in Norwich, where Ray Davies presented his new book *Americana* at a major book fair. We saw an entertaining two-hour interview with Ray about the book, mixed with him performing new songs! While waiting for the train back to London, it turned out that Ray and company also went back with the same train. I had a short chat with Ray, and I told him about the cancelled musical. He felt sorry for us, as we'd travelled so far without seeing the musical. He told us some good news: *Sunny Afternoon* would transfer to the West End and that we would get new tickets. Two months later, I received an email from Harald Pinter Theatre that said I would receive six tickets for the premiere of *Sunny Afternoon* on 4 October. Wow! An amazing musical and a fantastic man – Ray Davies!

Craig Davidson – Edmonds, Washington, US

In October 2014, my wife and I were living in Germany when *Sunny Afternoon* premiered in London's West End. Growing up in Canada – during the 1980s and 1990s – I never had the chance to see The Kinks live, so after we moved to Europe, seeing Ray's musical became my white whale. When the show moved to the Harold Pinter Theatre, I stayed up all night to buy tickets (first row, balcony, opening night of the previews). The itinerary was simple: fly in from Nuremberg at 10 am, see the show at 7:30 pm, then head back to the airport for a 6 am return flight. There was no time for sleep – this was The Kinks!

After landing in London, we gazed at Waterloo Bridge, saw Piccadilly, rambled and roamed around Soho (but not Pimlico) and Saville Row, and ate dinner at a restaurant across from the theatre (inadvertently crashing a pre-show celebration being held by some of the cast and their parents). Seated in the balcony, we filled our phones with pictures – getting an eerie feeling we were being judged – and watched as a man wearing a black fedora came in, said hello to our seatmates and sat behind us. At first, I thought it was Dave Davies, but I couldn't tell in the dim light. My wife urged me to turn around and say hello, but I didn't want to be rude – and I didn't know what to say. The only thing I could think of was, 'Your music changed my life', but I knew that was too inadequate to convey what The Kinks meant to me. I needed Dave to know that his music didn't just change my life; it defined who I was. By the intermission, I was a nervous wreck. While I thought I might see Ray or Dave, I never thought I'd actually have a chat. So, preoccupied with what I'd say, I headed to the cloakroom to burn off some anxiety while my wife tried to find Dave (who had vanished into thin air).

The conversation I planned was majestic. I wanted to start by nonchalantly telling him that 'Come Dancing' captured my attention in 1983, but *Misfits* and *Sleepwalker* – the next two albums I bought – turned me into a fan. Then, once the small talk was out of the way, I'd pivot into thanking him for writing 'You Don't Know My Name', as it filled a void in my soul and made me feel understood (I never had any real friends because we moved around a lot when I was a kid), and I'd tell him how 'Trust Your Heart' played in my brain every time I made a decision that strayed from the norm. I'd casually mention that my respect for his musicality grew after I read *Kink* and realised how instrumental he was to Ray's creative process. (I might have even commiserated about controlling older brothers by telling him that mine almost scuttled my 14th birthday present – *State Of Confusion* – because he thought The Kinks weren't my 'kind of band.') And I would have ended by eloquently expressing my heartfelt gratitude for giving me – an unsure-of-himself, preppy-rebel-adolescent outsider – the music that became the soundtrack of my life. I just hoped I wouldn't cry (but I was sure I would).

Unfortunately, it never happened. In the cloakroom, one of the parents burst my bubble by telling me how he'd ferreted out a balcony-inhabiting, fedora-wearing, superfan-doppelganger – who apparently confessed to his lack of notoriety with 'I'm just a fan of The Kinks' when asked if he was a Davies. Crestfallen, I said no to an invitation to the afterparty, found my wife (who was still fruitlessly searching for Dave) and waited for the second act. About halfway through, I decided to avoid a life of regret by finding out the truth myself, but once the lights came up, the mystery man was nowhere to be found.

A few days later, my Facebook feed made me realise I should have thrown my Canadian politeness aside, taken a chance, shown a little bit of emotion and gushed like the fan I am. Not only had Dave been our seatmate, but he had also attended the afterparty, and we had been sitting among the cast of characters Ray famously called out in the song 'The Moneygoround' (explaining why Dave seemed to know them and why they looked at us like interlopers). But, as they say, life goes on. God save The Kinks.

2015
Around The Dial With ... Jonathan Lea

After Ray joined Dave and the band for 'You Really Got Me' at the Islington Assembly Hall on 18 December 2015, I received hundreds of requests to tell my version of the events leading to their reunion.

At rehearsal on Thursday, Dave (who had the flu) casually mentioned that he'd asked Ray to join him onstage at the show the following evening. I really didn't think it would happen and had forgotten about it by the time we arrived at the venue the next afternoon.

During the show, 'Young And Innocent Days' featured Dave with Tom Currier on piano, so I left the stage to stand in the wings. There was a tall man standing on stage left when I got there, but I couldn't see his face. A few seconds later, he turned to me, and I realised it was Ray. He was very friendly, and we chatted through my entire break, with him asking me how Dave was doing and how the US tour went. When the song finished, I immediately told drummer Dennis Diken, 'Ray's here', and I managed to tell Tom a few songs later. I waited until the very end, when we were going to play 'You Really Got Me' as the final encore, to tell Dave so that it would just happen spontaneously. When he introduced Ray, the reaction was incredible. I'd never seen or heard that kind of gasping, screaming and excitement except in The Beatles film *A Hard Day's Night*. Ray went to use my microphone (stage right) and I directed him to use Dave's microphone centre stage. Ray asked Dave if that was okay. Dave then started his riff to 'You Really Got Me' and Ray jumped right in. It felt amazing. During Dave's solo, Ray turned to me, smiled and nodded, which I interpreted as him saying, 'This rocks!'

It was all over very quickly, and as soon as we left the stage, we were asked by Ray's assistant if Ray could join us in the band's dressing room. We, of course, said yes. He entered a minute or two later, very friendly and extremely complimentary, telling us numerous times that Dave had a 'great band.' I got him a Grolsch, and we discussed Dave's recent tour (he was aware that I'd missed a show due to an extreme medical emergency). Even though he'd told others, 'no photos', he happily agreed to pose for photos with the band and then he was off. A day I'll remember all my life.

Lea is a Grammy Award-nominated guitarist from Los Angeles who has worked with many legendary artists, including tours with Dave Davies from 2000 to 2015.

2018
Vincent de Waal – Baarn, The Netherlands

Sometimes, it takes a bit of coincidence to run into Ray Davies, Mick Avory and Dave Davies. It happened to me when I was in London and visiting an exhibit about the album *The Kinks Are The Village Green Preservation Society*. Upon entering the Proud Galleries, not far from Trafalgar Square, ITV cameras were there and reporter Nina Nannar and her crew waited to meet the band. Not much later, Ray, Mick and Dave stepped inside.

During Nannar's interview with Ray Davies, she presented him with a gold record. Fifty years after the LP was released, more than 100,000 of them had been sold in Britain. Naturally, Mick and Dave also received a gold record. This also explained why, a moment before, I had seen Ray arrive with a large Marks & Spencer bag.

The Kinks released the *Village Green* LP in November 1968, and it became the last album from the original lineup: Ray Davies, Dave Davies, Pete Quaife and Mick Avory. In honour of the 50th anniversary, the Proud exhibit featured commissioned artworks by band members (especially Dave Davies) and vintage memorabilia, along with photographs from this period of the band. Many works were signed by Ray, Dave and Mick.

The exhibit included images from the photo shoot of the album's artwork in Hampstead Heath, captured by music photojournalist Barrie Wentzell. The original quartet sat on the grass against the historic backdrop of Kenwood House, which Wentzell has said was Ray's favourite location.

Finally, the *Village Green* LP got the appreciation it deserved. A headline in *The Guardian* above an article about the exhibit said, 'First a flop – now a classic'. It was a special moment because it's not often that the three remaining band members from the first lineup get together. At the opening of the exhibit in early October were all kinds of guests, including Wentzell.

The item broadcast on ITV News that night lasted only two and a half minutes and can be seen on YouTube. Ray tells Nina Nannar that the *Village Green* album 'was about celebrating the small things in life. You can't live in the past all the time. Just move forward. Appreciate the past and take it with you.' And upon receiving the gold record: 'This is like what they give somebody when they retire. Except it's from my fans.' Of course, he mentioned that there were plans to make a theatrical version of the album, but nothing was heard of that afterwards.

Before the interview began, the few regular visitors had to leave the galleries. Through the window, I was able to take pictures. At the end of the meeting, a photographer took another picture of Ray, Dave and Mick (with their gold records) together with people from the record company (BMG) and from the Proud Galleries. Standing next to that photographer, I also took a picture of this company.

A little later, I spoke to Ray outside the galleries. We'd met twice before, first in Utrecht in The Netherlands and later at Konk Studios in London, and he recognised me. I asked Nina Nannar if she would take a picture of both of us.

Whether Ray ended up carrying the gold record in his M&S bag, I'll never know.

The 2020s (So Far)

In early 2021, a one-man performance called *The Moneygoround* streamed for one night only on The Kinks' YouTube channel. Written by Ray Davies and playwright Paul Sirett, it drew inspiration from the *Lola Versus Powerman And The Moneygoround* album released 50 years earlier. That December, BBC Radio 4 aired *Lola Vs. Powerman*, also by Davies and Sirett, which covered similar ground.

Dave Davies published a second memoir, *Living On A Thin Line*, in mid-2022. The book revisited The Kinks' early days but with different stories than 1996's *Kink*, and then it brought the narrative to the present, including his 2004 stroke and recovery. A new compilation of Dave's music with the same title accompanied the book's release.

In March 2023, The Kinks kicked off their 60th anniversary with the release of *The Journey – Part 1*, a new compilation of hits and lesser-known songs organised under different themes and weaved together with new liner notes from the band. Also that month, an invitation-only event for fans, family and friends – attended by Ray, Dave and Mick Avory – celebrated the band's six decades.

Keyboard player John Gosling died in August 2023 at the age of 75.

In September, The Kinks joined the Camden Music Walk of Fame with a ceremony that Mick attended. Actors John Dalgliesh and George Maguire – who played Ray and Dave in the *Sunny Afternoon* musical – performed a selection of Kinks songs and shared messages from the Davies brothers.

The Journey – Part 2 was released in November 2023.

In 2024, the Chicago Shakespeare Theater announced it would stage the first US production of the *Sunny Afternoon* musical in the spring of 2025.

Rumours of a Kinks reunion still appear periodically in the press.

Afterword: 2023

> Some of my songs have secret signals in them. I am a shy person, so many people who like or get what I do seem like they are part of a secret society.
> From a Ray Davies interview (circa 2010)

In Kinks lore, 6 Denmark Terrace in Muswell Hill – Ray and Dave Davies' childhood home – has become an almost mythical place. In the front room, their family held raucous parties that usually lasted into the wee hours of the morning, teaching the Davies boys about the joys of entertaining others. The brothers later collaborated there on many of the early hits – Ray has said those moments were the closest he felt to God and religion while growing up.

Directly across the street is The Clissold Arms, the neighbourhood pub where Ray and Dave first performed publicly in 1960. From the outside, it looks like one of the hundreds of gastropubs around London today, although with a Greek flair.

If you didn't know their history, you might walk past without giving either of them a second look. It's an apt metaphor for The Kinks' best work, which elevates ordinary people and places into something extraordinary – fleeting moments frozen forever in unforgettable three- or four-minute pop songs.

Although I have been a rampant Anglophile for as long as I can remember, I've only been able to visit London three times in my life – but each time, I have made the pilgrimage to the Fortis Green neighbourhood, paused for a while at Denmark Terrace and tried to imagine the working-class upbringing that fed the young Davies brothers' thirst for music.

After years of different owners embracing and then downplaying its importance in rock 'n' roll history, the latest management team at The Clissold has an entire Kinks-themed room filled with art and memorabilia from throughout the band's remarkable history. The pub also hosts regular performances celebrating The Kinks' legendary songbook, and none is more important (at least in my opinion!) than the Kinksfan Kollectiv's annual sing-along night.

For more than a decade (with roots stretching back even further), the Kollectiv has performed at The Clissold and other North London pubs on the night before the Official Kinks Fan Club Meeting in late November. Organiser and all-around gent Geoff Lewis pulls together fans from all over the world (with help from Olga Ruocco, Ian Rhydderch and others) for an eclectic set of hits and deep cuts.

Because they're from the US, the UK, The Netherlands and elsewhere, members of the Kollectiv learn the songs from Kinks recordings and don't get a chance to rehearse together before the gig. Is everything note-perfect? Of course not, but we all appreciate the love that goes into the performance. Everyone in the audience knows all the words and is unashamed to belt 'em out as loudly and enthusiastically as possible.

Both Ray and Dave have attended the Kollectiv's sing-along nights over the years, as have other members of The Kinks. Harkening back to the early years, Ray once said: 'My songs were written when I lived opposite a pub, where I grew up. I always wanted them to be heard in a pub, and lo and behold, I've achieved my ambition!' A little facetious, perhaps, but there's a ring of truth: he's admitted elsewhere that he felt success when 'Sunny Afternoon' and other songs got a good reaction around the piano in the front room.

At the November 2023 sing-along, I found myself perched at the top of the stairs between the bar and Kinks Room, where the band performed, so I had a good view of both the music and the crowd. Many of them were Facebook friends or contributors to this book (often both), and a few – like Olga and Geoff – I've known for more than half my life.

Maybe it's because Ray and Dave are brothers, but the Kinks fandom feels more like a family. Sure, sometimes it's a dysfunctional family, but ultimately, we stick together to try to get the band the recognition they deserve for their groundbreaking work.

New fans are like distant cousins we haven't met yet, and we happily welcome them into the fold. I spent some time at the Kollectiv sing-along chatting with a 17-year-old fan who had just discovered The Kinks a few months earlier, and I'm sure that enthusiasm like hers will keep the music alive for generations to come.

Although we're never all in the same room, our shared love for the songs is what brings Kinks fans together – the outsiders, the misfits, the loners and the ones who never could quite fit in. We've heard the secret signals, and they speak directly to our hearts.

Chris Kocher, Editor
March 2024

Also available from Sonicbond

The Hollies – on track
Every album, every song

Andrew Darlington
Paperback
160 pages
48 colour photographs
978-1-78951-159-7
£14.99
$21.95

Every album by these British pop legends.

'The road is long, with many a winding turn, that leads us to who knows where? Who knows where?'

Everyone loved The Hollies. They were the 'group's group'. Never confrontational or rebellious, always smartly suited, always smiling. The band had an unbroken run of immaculate pop singles which, while they seldom had that must-buy factor of the latest Rolling Stones or Beatles record, were hallmarked by tight harmonies and an almost unfailing chart sensibility. Throughout the sixties and well into the seventies, everyone had at least one or two Hollies singles in their collection and nobody begrudged The Hollies their hits.

When 'He Ain't Heavy, He's My Brother' and 'Long Cool Woman In A Black Dress' became global million-sellers, The Hollies were inducted into The Rock 'n' Roll Hall Of Fame. Graham Nash – by then deep into his second career as part of Crosby, Stills and Nash - was reunited with other members of the outfit on stage together in the March 2010 ceremony.

This book tells the full story of the band's music, from the band's origins in Manchester, through the full arc of hits, and the albums – track-by-track, into the twenty-first century, then … now … always.

Also available from Sonicbond

The Kinks – on track
Every album, every song

Martin Hutchinson
Paperback
160 pages
47 colour photographs
978-1-78951-172-6
£15.99
$21.95

Every album by this hugely-influential London-based group.

Hailing from Muswell Hill in London, The Kinks were one of the top British bands of the sixties, with over twenty hit singles in the UK, including a trio of number ones, the famous tribute to their home city 'Waterloo Sunset' being one. They also had ten top thirty hits in the USA thanks to the clever and sometimes sardonic songwriting of Ray Davies, who dominated the band and deservedly went on to be knighted. When the seventies came along, they recorded a number of critically acclaimed concept albums, and their live shows became more theatrical, with the band shifting focus to become pioneers of arena rock in America. Following a resurgence of commercial popularity in the late seventies and early eighties, the band continued to record interesting and lyrically insightful albums. They last performed together in 1996.

The combination of Ray's songs and the musicianship of the band – including his brother Dave Davies, with whom Ray had a rather tempestuous relationship – has led to many bands citing them as an influence. This book examines every track released by The Kinks, whether released on single or album, and provides a valuable insight into one of music's greatest groups.

Also available from Sonicbond

On Track Series

AC/DC – Chris Sutton 978-1-78952-307-2

Allman Brothers Band – Andrew Wild 978-1-78952-252-5

Tori Amos – Lisa Torem 978-1-78952-142-9

Aphex Twin – Beau Waddell 978-1-78952-267-9

Asia – Peter Braidis 978-1-78952-099-6

Badfinger – Robert Day-Webb 978-1-878952-176-4

Barclay James Harvest – Keith and Monica Domone 978-1-78952-067-5

Beck – Arthur Lizie 978-1-78952-258-7

The Beat, General Public, Fine Young Cannibals – Steve Parry 978-1-78952-274-7

The Beatles – Andrew Wild 978-1-78952-009-5

The Beatles Solo 1969-1980 – Andrew Wild 978-1-78952-030-9

Blue Oyster Cult – Jacob Holm-Lupo 978-1-78952-007-1

Blur – Matt Bishop 978-178952-164-1

Marc Bolan and T.Rex – Peter Gallagher 978-1-78952-124-5

Kate Bush – Bill Thomas 978-1-78952-097-2

The Byrds – Andy McArthur 978-1-78952-280-8

Camel – Hamish Kuzminski 978-1-78952-040-8

Captain Beefheart – Opher Goodwin 978-1-78952-235-8

Caravan – Andy Boot 978-1-78952-127-6

Cardiacs – Eric Benac 978-1-78952-131-3

Wendy Carlos – Mark Marrington 978-1-78952-331-7

The Carpenters – Paul Tornbohm 978-1-78952-301-0

Nick Cave and The Bad Seeds – Dominic Sanderson 978-1-78952-240-2

Eric Clapton Solo – Andrew Wild 978-1-78952-141-2

The Clash – Nick Assirati 978-1-78952-077-4

Elvis Costello and The Attractions – Georg Purvis 978-1-78952-129-0

Crosby, Stills and Nash – Andrew Wild 978-1-78952-039-2

Creedence Clearwater Revival – Tony Thompson 978-178952-237-2

The Damned – Morgan Brown 978-1-78952-136-8

David Bowie 1964 to 1982 – Carl Ewens 978-1-78952-324-9

Deep Purple and Rainbow 1968-79 – Steve Pilkington 978-1-78952-002-6

Depeche Mode – Brian J. Robb 978-1-78952-277-8

Also available from Sonicbond

Dire Straits – Andrew Wild 978-1-78952-044-6

The Divine Comedy – Alan Draper 978-1-78952-308-9

The Doors – Tony Thompson 978-1-78952-137-5

Dream Theater – Jordan Blum 978-1-78952-050-7

Bob Dylan 1962-1970 – Opher Goodwin 978-1-78952-275-2

Eagles – John Van der Kiste 978-1-78952-260-0

Earth, Wind and Fire – Bud Wilkins 978-1-78952-272-3

Electric Light Orchestra – Barry Delve 978-1-78952-152-8

Emerson Lake and Palmer – Mike Goode 978-1-78952-000-2

Fairport Convention – Kevan Furbank 978-1-78952-051-4

Peter Gabriel – Graeme Scarfe 978-1-78952-138-2

Genesis – Stuart MacFarlane 978-1-78952-005-7

Gentle Giant – Gary Steel 978-1-78952-058-3

Gong – Kevan Furbank 978-1-78952-082-8

Green Day – William E. Spevack 978-1-78952-261-7

Steve Hackett – Geoffrey Feakes 978-1-78952-098-9

Hall and Oates – Ian Abrahams 978-1-78952-167-2

Peter Hammill – Richard Rees Jones 978-1-78952-163-4

Roy Harper – Opher Goodwin 978-1-78952-130-6

Hawkwind (new edition) – Duncan Harris 978-1-78952-290-7

Jimi Hendrix – Emma Stott 978-1-78952-175-7

The Hollies – Andrew Darlington 978-1-78952-159-7

Horslips – Richard James 978-1-78952-263-1

The Human League and The Sheffield Scene – Andrew Darlington 978-1-78952-186-3

Humble Pie –Robert Day-Webb 978-1-78952-2761

Ian Hunter – G. Mick Smith 978-1-78952-304-1

The Incredible String Band – Tim Moon 978-1-78952-107-8

INXS – Manny Grillo 978-1-78952-302-7

Iron Maiden – Steve Pilkington 978-1-78952-061-3

Joe Jackson – Richard James 978-1-78952-189-4

The Jam – Stan Jeffries 978-1-78952-299-0

Jefferson Airplane – Richard Butterworth 978-1-78952-143-6

Jethro Tull – Jordan Blum 978-1-78952-016-3

Elton John in the 1970s – Peter Kearns 978-1-78952-034-7

Also available from Sonicbond

Billy Joel – Lisa Torem 978-1-78952-183-2
Judas Priest – John Tucker 978-1-78952-018-7
Kansas – Kevin Cummings 978-1-78952-057-6
Killing Joke – Nic Ransome 978-1-78952-273-0
The Kinks – Martin Hutchinson 978-1-78952-172-6
Korn – Matt Karpe 978-1-78952-153-5
Led Zeppelin – Steve Pilkington 978-1-78952-151-1
Level 42 – Matt Philips 978-1-78952-102-3
Little Feat – Georg Purvis – 978-1-78952-168-9
Magnum – Matthew Taylor – 978-1-78952-286-0
Aimee Mann – Jez Rowden 978-1-78952-036-1
Ralph McTell – Paul O. Jenkins 978-1-78952-294-5
Metallica – Barry Wood 978-1-78952-269-3
Joni Mitchell – Peter Kearns 978-1-78952-081-1
The Moody Blues – Geoffrey Feakes 978-1-78952-042-2
Motorhead – Duncan Harris 978-1-78952-173-3
Nektar – Scott Meze – 978-1-78952-257-0
New Order – Dennis Remmer – 978-1-78952-249-5
Nightwish – Simon McMurdo – 978-1-78952-270-9
Nirvana – William E. Spevack 978-1-78952-318-8
Laura Nyro – Philip Ward 978-1-78952-182-5
Oasis – 978-1-78952-300-3
Mike Oldfield – Ryan Yard 978-1-78952-060-6
Opeth – Jordan Blum 978-1-78-952-166-5
Pearl Jam – Ben L. Connor 978-1-78952-188-7
Tom Petty – Richard James 978-1-78952-128-3
Pink Floyd – Richard Butterworth 978-1-78952-242-6
The Police – Pete Braidis 978-1-78952-158-0
Porcupine Tree – Nick Holmes 978-1-78952-144-3
Procol Harum – Scott Meze 978-1-78952-315-7
Queen – Andrew Wild 978-1-78952-003-3
Radiohead – William Allen 978-1-78952-149-8
Rancid – Paul Matts 978-1-78952-187-0
Lou Reed 1972-1986 – Ethan Roy 978-1-78952-283-9

Also available from Sonicbond

Renaissance – David Detmer 978-1-78952-062-0

REO Speedwagon – Jim Romag 978-1-78952-262-4

The Rolling Stones 1963-80 – Steve Pilkington 978-1-78952-017-0

Linda Ronstadt 1969-1989 – Daryl O. Lawrence 987-1-78952-293-8

Sensational Alex Harvey Band – Peter Gallagher 978-1-7952-289-1

The Small Faces and The Faces – Andrew Darlington 978-1-78952-316-4

The Smashing Pumpkins – Matt Karpe 978-1-7952-291-4

The Smiths and Morrissey – Tommy Gunnarsson 978-1-78952-140-5

Spirit – Rev. Keith A. Gordon – 978-1-78952- 248-8

Soft Machine – Scott Meze 978-1078952-271-6

Stackridge – Alan Draper 978-1-78952-232-7

Status Quo the Frantic Four Years – Richard James 978-1-78952-160-3

Steely Dan – Jez Rowden 978-1-78952-043-9

The Stranglers – Martin Hutchinson 978-1-78952-323-2

Talk Talk – Gary Steel 978-1-78952-284-6

Tears For Fears – Paul Clark – 978-178952-238-9

Thin Lizzy – Graeme Stroud 978-1-78952-064-4

Tool – Matt Karpe 978-1-78952-234-1

Toto – Jacob Holm-Lupo 978-1-78952-019-4

U2 – Eoghan Lyng 978-1-78952-078-1

UFO – Richard James 978-1-78952-073-6

Ultravox – Brian J. Robb 978-1-78952-330-0

Van Der Graaf Generator – Dan Coffey 978-1-78952-031-6

Van Halen – Morgan Brown – 9781-78952-256-3

Suzanne Vega – Lisa Torem 978-1-78952-281-5

Jack White And The White Stripes – Ben L. Connor 978-1-78952-303-4

The Who – Geoffrey Feakes 978-1-78952-076-7

Roy Wood and the Move – James R Turner 978-1-78952-008-8

Yes (new edition) – Stephen Lambe 978-1-78952-282-2

Neil Young 1963 to 1970 – Oper Goodwin 978-1-78952-298-3

Frank Zappa 1966 to 1979 – Eric Benac 978-1-78952-033-0

Warren Zevon – Peter Gallagher 978-1-78952-170-2

The Zombies – Emma Stott 978-1-78952-297-6

10CC – Peter Kearns 978-1-78952-054-5

Decades Series

The Bee Gees in the 1960s – Andrew Mon Hughes et al 978-1-78952-148-1

The Bee Gees in the 1970s – Andrew Mon Hughes et al 978-1-78952-179-5

Black Sabbath in the 1970s – Chris Sutton 978-1-78952-171-9

Britpop – Peter Richard Adams and Matt Pooler 978-1-78952-169-6

Phil Collins in the 1980s – Andrew Wild 978-1-78952-185-6

Alice Cooper in the 1970s – Chris Sutton 978-1-78952-104-7

Alice Cooper in the 1980s – Chris Sutton 978-1-78952-259-4

Curved Air in the 1970s – Laura Shenton 978-1-78952-069-9

Donovan in the 1960s – Jeff Fitzgerald 978-1-78952-233-4

Bob Dylan in the 1980s – Don Klees 978-1-78952-157-3

Brian Eno in the 1970s – Gary Parsons 978-1-78952-239-6

Faith No More in the 1990s – Matt Karpe 978-1-78952-250-1

Fleetwood Mac in the 1970s – Andrew Wild 978-1-78952-105-4

Fleetwood Mac in the 1980s – Don Klees 978-178952-254-9

Focus in the 1970s – Stephen Lambe 978-1-78952-079-8

Free and Bad Company in the 1970s – John Van der Kiste 978-1-78952-178-8

Genesis in the 1970s – Bill Thomas 978178952-146-7

George Harrison in the 1970s – Eoghan Lyng 978-1-78952-174-0

Kiss in the 1970s – Peter Gallagher 978-1-78952-246-4

Manfred Mann's Earth Band in the 1970s –
John Van der Kiste 978178952-243-3

Marillion in the 1980s – Nathaniel Webb 978-1-78952-065-1

Van Morrison in the 1970s – Peter Childs – 978-1-78952-241-9

Mott the Hoople & Ian Hunter in the 1970s –
John Van der Kiste 978-1-78-952-162-7

Pink Floyd In The 1970s – Georg Purvis 978-1-78952-072-9

Suzi Quatro in the 1970s – Darren Johnson 978-1-78952-236-5

Queen in the 1970s – James Griffiths 978-1-78952-265-5

Roxy Music in the 1970s – Dave Thompson 978-1-78952-180-1

Slade in the 1970s – Darren Johnson 978-1-78952-268-6

Status Quo in the 1980s – Greg Harper 978-1-78952-244-0

Tangerine Dream in the 1970s – Stephen Palmer 978-1-78952-161-0

The Sweet in the 1970s – Darren Johnson 978-1-78952-139-9

Uriah Heep in the 1970s – Steve Pilkington 978-1-78952-103-0

Van der Graaf Generator in the 1970s – Steve Pilkington 978-1-78952-245-7
Rick Wakeman in the 1970s – Geoffrey Feakes 978-1-78952-264-8
Yes in the 1980s – Stephen Lambe with David Watkinson 978-1-78952-125-2

Rock Classics Series

90125 by Yes – Stephen Lambe 978-1-78952-329-4
Bat Out Of Hell by Meatloaf – Geoffrey Feakes 978-1-78952-320-1
Bringing It All Back Home by Bob Dylan – Opher Goodwin 978-1-78952-314-0
Crime Of The Century by Supertramp – Steve Pilkington 978-1-78952-327-0
Let It Bleed by The Rolling Stones – John Van der Kiste 978-1-78952-309-6
Purple Rain by Prince – Matt Karpe 978-1-78952-322-5

On Screen Series

Carry On... – Stephen Lambe 978-1-78952-004-0
David Cronenberg – Patrick Chapman 978-1-78952-071-2
Doctor Who: The David Tennant Years – Jamie Hailstone 978-1-78952-066-8
James Bond – Andrew Wild 978-1-78952-010-1
Monty Python – Steve Pilkington 978-1-78952-047-7
Seinfeld Seasons 1 to 5 – Stephen Lambe 978-1-78952-012-5

Other Books

1967: A Year In Psychedelic Rock 978-1-78952-155-9
1970: A Year In Rock – John Van der Kiste 978-1-78952-147-4
1972: The Year Progressive Rock Ruled The World – Kevan Furbank 978-1-78952-288-4
1973: The Golden Year of Progressive Rock 978-1-78952-165-8
Babysitting A Band On The Rocks – G.D. Praetorius 978-1-78952-106-1
Eric Clapton Sessions – Andrew Wild 978-1-78952-177-1
Dark Horse Records – Aaron Badgley 978-1-78952-287-7
Derek Taylor: For Your Radioactive Children – Andrew Darlington 978-1-78952-038-5
The Golden Age of Easy Listening – Derek Taylor 978-1-78952-285-3
The Golden Road: The Recording History of The Grateful Dead – John Kilbride 978-1-78952-156-6

Iggy and The Stooges On Stage 1967-1974 – Per Nilsen 978-1-78952-101-6

Jon Anderson and the Warriors – the road to Yes – David Watkinson 978-1-78952-059-0

Magic: The David Paton Story – David Paton 978-1-78952-266-2

Misty: The Music of Johnny Mathis – Jakob Baekgaard 978-1-78952-247-1

Nu Metal: A Definitive Guide – Matt Karpe 978-1-78952-063-7

Remembering Live Aid – Andrew Wild 978-1-78952-328-7

Tommy Bolin: In and Out of Deep Purple – Laura Shenton 978-1-78952-070-5

Maximum Darkness – Deke Leonard 978-1-78952-048-4

The Twang Dynasty – Deke Leonard 978-1-78952-049-1

And Many More To Come!

Would you like to write for Sonicbond Publishing?

At Sonicbond Publishing we are always on the look-out for authors, particularly for our two main series:

On Track. Mixing fact with in depth analysis, the On Track series examines the work of a particular musical artist or group. All genres are considered from easy listening and jazz to 60s soul to 90s pop, via rock and metal.

On Screen. This series looks at the world of film and television. Subjects considered include directors, actors and writers, as well as entire television and film series. As with the On Track series, we balance fact with analysis.

While professional writing experience would, of course, be an advantage the most important qualification is to have real enthusiasm and knowledge of your subject. First-time authors are welcomed, but the ability to write well in English is essential.

Sonicbond Publishing has distribution throughout Europe and North America, and all books are also published in E-book form. Authors will be paid a royalty based on sales of their book.

Further details are available from www.sonicbondpublishing.co.uk. To contact us, complete the contact form there or
email info@sonicbondpublishing.co.uk